Rick Steves

POCKET

VENICE

Rick Steves & Gene Openshaw

Contents

Introduction

Venice is a world apart. Built on a hundred islands, its exotic-looking palaces are laced together by graceful bridges over sun-speckled canals. Romantics revel in the city's atmosphere of elegant decay. And first-time visitors are often stirred deeply, waking from their ordinary lives to a fantasy world unlike anything they've ever seen.

Those are strong reactions, considering that Venice today, frankly, can also be an overcrowded tourist trap. But Venice offers so much. By day, it's a city of art-filled museums, trendy shops, and narrow alleyways. At night, when the hordes of day-trippers have gone, another Venice appears. Glide in a gondola through quiet canals. Don a Carnevale mask—or just a fresh shirt—and become someone else for a night.

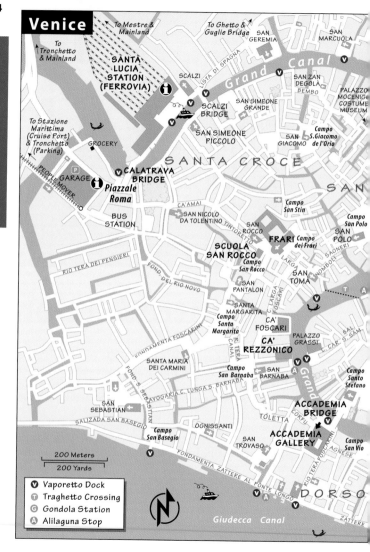

Venice

To Mestre & Mainland

To Ghetto & Guglie Bridge

SAN GEREMIA

SAN MARCUOLA

To Tronchetto & Mainland

SANTA LUCIA STATION (FERROVIA)

SCALZI

LISTA DI SPAGNA

Grand Canal

SAN ZAN DEGOLA

BEMBO

PALAZZO MOCENIGO COSTUME MUSEUM

SCALZI BRIDGE

SAN SIMEONE GRANDE

SAN GIACOMO

Campo S.Giacomo de l'Orio

To Stazione Marittima (Cruise Port) & Tronchetto (Parking)

SAN SIMEONE PICCOLO

GROCERY

SANTA CROCE

SAN

People Mover

GARAGE

CALATRAVA BRIDGE

Piazzale Roma

CA'AMAI

SAN NICOLO DA TOLENTINO

TINTORETTO

SAN ROCCO

Campo San Stin

Campo San Polo

SAN POLO

BUS STATION

FRARI

Campo dei Frari

RIO TERA DEI PENSIERI

FOND. DEL RIO NOVO

SCUOLA SAN ROCCO

Campo San Rocco

SAONERI

LARGA

SAN TOMA

NOMBOLI

SAN PANTALON

SANTA MARGARITA

C. LARGA FOSCARI

T A

FONDAMENTA FOSCARINI

Campo Santa Margarita

CA' FOSCARI

CA' REZZONICO

PALAZZO GRASSI

SANTA MARIA DEI CARMINI

R. TERA CANAL

FOND. S. SEBASTIAN

SAVOGNA C. LUNGA S. BARNABA

Campo San Barnaba

SAN BARNABA

SAL. CAF. S. SAM.

Grand

Campo Santo Stefano

SAN SEBASTIAN

SALIZADA SAN BASEGIO

TOLETTA

CORFU

ACCADEMIA BRIDGE

OGNISSANTI

Campo San Basegio

SAN TROVASO

ACCADEMIA GALLERY

RIO TERA FOSCARINI

Campo San Vio

FONDAMENTA ZATTERE AL PONTE LONGO

DORSO

200 Meters

200 Yards

V Vaporetto Dock
T Traghetto Crossing
G Gondola Station
A Alilaguna Stop

Giudecca Canal

ZATTERE

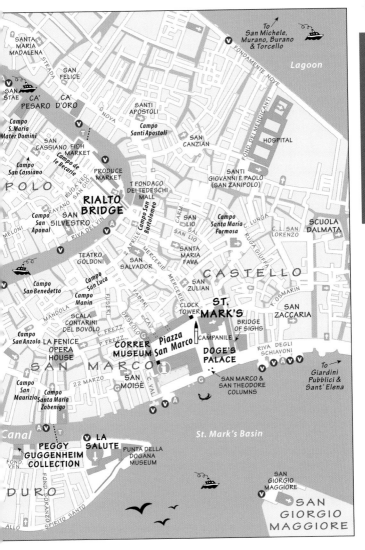

To San Michele, Murano, Burano & Torcello

Lagoon

SANTA MARIA MADALENA

STRADA

SAN FELICE

SAN STAE

CA' PESARO

CA' D'ORO

NOVA

SANTI APOSTOLI

FONDAMENTE NOVE

FOND. DEI MENDICANTI

Campo S.Maria Mater Domini

SAN CASSIANO

FISH MARKET

Campo de le Becarie

Campo Santi Apostoli

SAN CANZIAN

HOSPITAL

Campo San Cassiano

RUGA VECCHIA SAN GIO.

PRODUCE MARKET

SANTI GIOVANNI E PAOLO (SAN ZANIPOLO)

POLO

RAVANO

T FONDACO DEI TEDESCHI MALL

Campo Santa Maria Formosa

RUGA LUNGA

SCUOLA DALMATA

Campo San Silvestro

SAN POLO

RIALTO BRIDGE

Campo San Bartolomeo

SAN LIO

SAL SAN LIO

C. I. SAN LORENZO

MELONI

Campo San Aponal

RIVA DEL VIN

2 APRILE

MERCERIE

SANTA MARIA FAVA

RUGA GIUFFA

TEATRO GOLDONI

SAN SALVADOR

MERCERIE

CASTELLO

Campo San Benedetto

Campo San Luca

FABBRI

SAN ZULIAN

F. OSMARIN

Campo Manin

MANDOLA

ORSEOLO

MERCERIE

CLOCK TOWER

ST. MARK'S

SAN ZACCARIA

SCALA CONTARINI DEL BOVOLO

CAV.

BRIDGE OF SIGHS

Campo San Anzolo

LA FENICE OPERA HOUSE

P. FREZZ.

P. FREZZ.

CORRER MUSEUM

Piazza San Marco

CAMPANILE

DOGE'S PALACE

RIVA DEGLI SCHIAVONI

SAN MARCO

Campo San Maurizio

Campo Santa Maria Zobenigo

22 MARZO

SAN MOISÈ

C. VAL.

SAN MARCO & SAN THEODORE COLUMNS

To Giardini Pubblici & Sant' Elena

Canal

FOND. VEN.

PEGGY GUGGENHEIM COLLECTION

LA SALUTE

PUNTA DELLA DOGANA MUSEUM

St. Mark's Basin

DURO

FOND. SORANZO

SPIRITO SANTO

ALLO

SAN GIORGIO MAGGIORE

SAN GIORGIO MAGGIORE

About This Book

Rick Steves Pocket Venice is a personal tour guide...in your pocket. The core of the book is eight self-guided walks and tours that zero in on Venice's greatest sights and experiences.

My Grand Canal Cruise, snaking through the heart of the historic core, introduces you to this moist metropolis. Then hit St. Mark's Square, with its one-of-a-kind basilica and Doge's Palace. I've included several neighborhood walks that take you to major sights (Rialto Bridge) and out-of-the-way places (Frari Church).

The rest of this book is a traveler's tool kit, with my best advice on how to save money, plan your time, use public transportation, and avoid lines at the busiest sights. You'll also get recommendations on hotels, restaurants, and activities.

Venice by Neighborhood

The island city of Venice is shaped like a fish. The Grand Canal winds through the middle of the fish, starting at the mouth where people enter, passing under the Rialto Bridge, and ending at St. Mark's Square. The city has six districts:

San Marco: The bustling district surrounding St. Mark's Square has the most tourists and the most sights: St. Mark's Basilica, the Doge's Palace, Bridge of Sighs, Campanile bell tower, Correr art museum, and café orchestras on the square. Accommodations and eateries are plentiful.

Dorsoduro: This quiet neighborhood across a bridge from San Marco hosts sights along the Grand Canal: the Accademia (Venetian Renaissance art), modern art museums (Peggy Guggenheim Collection and Punta della Dogana), the iconic La Salute Church, and Ca' Rezzonico.

San Polo: This lively district has the graceful Rialto Bridge, busy produce and fish markets, exquisite Frari Church, and Scuola San Rocco (Tintoretto paintings). It's also dotted with *cicchetti* bars, restaurants, and accommodations.

Santa Croce: Across the canal from the train station, this area features modern art (at Ca' Pesaro) but is pretty plain.

Cannaregio: This district contains the controversial Calatrava Bridge, train station, and historic Jewish Ghetto (with museum and memorials).

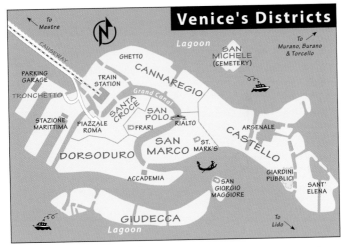

Venice's Districts

To Mestre

Lagoon

GHETTO

CANNAREGIO

CAUSEWAY

PARKING GARAGE

TRAIN STATION

TRONCHETTO

Grand Canal

SANTA CROCE

SAN POLO

FRARI

RIALTO

STAZIONE MARITTIMA

PIAZZALE ROMA

SAN MARCO

ST. MARK'S

DORSODURO

ACCADEMIA

SAN GIORGIO MAGGIORE

GIUDECCA

Lagoon

SAN MICHELE (CEMETERY)

To Murano, Burano & Torcello

ARSENALE

CASTELLO

GIARDINI PUBBLICI

SANT' ELENA

To Lido

Castello: Untouristy Castello has the picturesque Campo Santa Maria Formosa (with eateries nearby) and the slice-of-Venetian-life neighborhood along Via Garibaldi.

Venice's Lagoon: Beyond Venice are more islands. San Giorgio Maggiore, with its classic church, is a short vaporetto ride from St. Mark's Square. You can link other islands (San Michele, Murano, Burano, and Torcello) on a day trip.

Addresses generally list the district and house number (e.g., Cannaregio #221b), not the street. I find it easier to navigate by landmarks. Many street corners have a sign pointing you to *(per)* the nearest major landmark, such as San Marco, Accademia, Rialto, and Ferrovia (train station). I've organized this book—sights, hotels, and restaurants—around these major landmarks.

As you get more comfortable with the city, dare to disobey these signs and make your own discoveries. Escape the crowds and explore on foot. Don't worry about getting lost—in fact, get as lost as possible. Keep reminding yourself, "I'm on an island, and I can't get off." When it comes time to find your way, just follow the signs or simply ask a local, *"Dov'è San Marco?"* ("Where is St. Mark's?")

Venice at a Glance

▲▲▲**St. Mark's Square** Venice's grand main square. See page 31.

▲▲▲**St. Mark's Basilica** Cathedral with mosaics, saint's bones, treasury, museum, and viewpoint of square. **Hours:** Mon-Sat 9:30-17:00, Sun 14:00-17:00 (Sun until 16:30 Nov-Easter). See page 45.

▲▲▲**Doge's Palace** Art-splashed palace of former rulers, with prison accessible through Bridge of Sighs. **Hours:** Daily 9:00-18:00, off-season until 17:00. See page 65.

▲▲▲**Rialto Bridge** Distinctive bridge spanning the Grand Canal, with a market nearby. See page 141.

▲▲**Correr Museum** Venetian history and art. **Hours:** Daily 10:00-19:00, Nov-March 10:30-17:00. See page 128.

▲▲**Accademia** Venice's top art museum. **Hours:** Tue-Sun 8:15-19:15, Mon until 14:00. See page 134.

▲▲**Peggy Guggenheim Collection** Popular display of 20th-century art. **Hours:** Wed-Mon 10:00-18:00, closed Tue. See page 136.

▲▲**Frari Church** Franciscan church featuring Renaissance masters. **Hours:** Mon-Thu 9:00-19:30, Fri until 23:00, Sat until 18:00, Sun 13:00-18:00, shorter hours in winter. See page 83.

▲▲**Scuola San Rocco** "Tintoretto's Sistine Chapel." **Hours:** Daily 9:30-17:30. See page 143.

▲▲**Ca' Rezzonico** Posh Grand Canal palazzo with 18th-century Venetian art. **Hours:** Wed-Mon 10:00-18:00, Nov-March until 17:00, closed Tue year-round. See page 140.

Planning Your Time

The following day plans give an idea of how much an organized, motivated, and caffeinated person can see.

Plan your sightseeing carefully to avoid lines and work around closed days. (See my sightseeing tips on page 126.) Venice is small enough that, even if you only had one day, you could see the biggies in a 12-hour sightseeing blitz. But let's assume you have at least three days.

Day 1: In the morning, take the slow vaporetto #1 down the Grand Canal from the train station to St. Mark's. Ride to the top of

▲**Campanile** Dramatic bell tower on St. Mark's Square with elevator to the top. **Hours:** Daily roughly 9:30-20:45, shorter hours off-season. See page 131.

▲**Bridge of Sighs** Famous enclosed bridge, part of Doge's Palace, near St. Mark's Square. See page 43.

▲**La Salute Church** Striking church dedicated to the Virgin Mary. **Hours:** Daily 9:00-12:00 & 15:00-17:30, winter from 9:30. See page 139.

▲**Punta della Dogana** Museum of contemporary art. **Hours:** Wed-Mon 10:00-19:00, closed Tue. See page 140.

▲**Ca' Pesaro International Gallery of Modern Art** Fine museum in a canalside palazzo. **Hours:** Tue-Sun 10:00-18:00, Nov-March until 17:00, closed Mon year-round. See page 145.

▲**T Fondaco dei Tedeschi View Terrace** Rooftop terrace atop luxury mall, with views over the Grand Canal. **Hours:** Daily 10:30-18:30, June-Aug until 20:15, Nov-March until 19:15. See page 141.

▲**Scuola Dalmata di SS Giorgio e Trifone** Exquisite Renaissance meeting house. **Hours:** Mon 13:30-17:30, Tue-Sat 9:30-17:30, Sun 9:30-13:30. See page 148.

▲**Via Garibaldi** Walkable residential area with welcoming restaurants, parks, and shops. See page 149.

Church of San Zaccaria Final resting place of St. Zechariah, plus a Bellini altarpiece and an eerie crypt. **Hours:** Mon-Sat 10:00-12:00 & 16:00-18:00, Sun 16:00-18:00. See page 118.

the Campanile, and then take my self-guided St. Mark's Square Tour. Consider taking my St. Mark's to Rialto Loop Walk, then grab lunch at the *cicchetti* bars near the Rialto market. Spend the afternoon sightseeing the Correr Museum, the basilica, and the Doge's Palace. Around 19:00, have dinner (make a reservation). Afterward, enjoy the dueling orchestras with a drink on St. Mark's Square.

Day 2: Spend the morning shopping and exploring (consider my Rialto to Frari Church Walk) as you make your way to the Frari Church. See the Frari and head over to the Accademia/Dorsoduro area and have

lunch. Spend the afternoon seeing the Dorsoduro's main artsy sights: Ca' Rezzonico, Accademia, and the Peggy Guggenheim Collection. Around 18:00, do a *cicchetti* pub crawl for dinner. Afterward, take a gondola ride (or, much cheaper, a moonlight vaporetto ride).

Day 3 and Beyond: Choose from among Venice's lesser sights: a trip to San Giorgio Maggiore, La Salute, modern art at the Punta della Dogana, or the area east of St. Mark's (Church of San Zaccaria, Scuola Dalmata di San Giorgio). Budget time for just exploring, using my walks as a jumping-off point. In the evening, have dinner and catch a Vivaldi concert. With more time in Venice, you could visit the lagoon islands (Murano, Burano, and more), but these require at least a half-day.

Remember that Venice itself is its greatest sight. Make time to wander, explore, shop, and simply be. When you cross a bridge, look both ways. You may be hit with a lovely view.

When to Go

Venice's best travel months (also its busiest and most expensive) are April, May, June, September, and October.

Summer in Venice is more temperate (high 70s and 80s) than in Italy's scorching inland cities. Most Venetian hotels come with

Rick's Free Video Clips and Audio Tours

Rick Steves Classroom Europe, a powerful tool for teachers, is also useful for travelers. This video library contains about 500 short clips excerpted from my public television series. Enjoy these videos as you sort through options for your trip and to better understand what you'll see in Europe. Check it out at Classroom.RickSteves.com (just enter a topic to find everything I've filmed on a subject).

   Rick Steves Audio Europe, a free app, makes it easy to download my audio tours and listen to them offline as you travel. For this book (look for the 🎧), these audio tours include my Grand Canal Cruise and tours of the Frari Church, St. Mark's Basilica, and St. Mark's Square. The app also offers interviews (organized by country) from my public radio show with experts from Europe and around the globe. Find it in your app store or at RickSteves.com/AudioEurope.

air-conditioning, but it's usually available only from May (at the earliest) through September. Spring and fall can be cool, and many hotels are not allowed to turn on their heat until winter.

   In the off-season (November through March), you can usually expect mild winter weather (with lows in the 30s and 40s) and fewer tourists (except during the Carnevale festival in February).

   Here are several things to keep in mind if you visit Venice during that time:

- Most sights close early, often at 17:00.
- The orchestras in St. Mark's Square may stop playing at 18:00 (and may not play at all in bad weather or during their annual vacations, usually in March).
- Vaporetto service on the Grand Canal is reduced to the slow boat, vaporetto #1, which makes every stop along the way. The faster #2 boat is reduced to a shuttle route between Piazzale Roma, Ferrovia (train station), and Rialto.
- Expect occasional flooding, particularly at St. Mark's Square.

Before You Go

You'll have a smoother trip if you tackle a few things ahead of time. For more details on these topics, see the Practicalities chapter and RickSteves.com, which has helpful travel-tip articles and videos.

Make sure your travel documents are valid. If your passport is due to expire within six months of your ticketed date of return, you need to renew it. Allow six weeks or more to renew or get a passport (www.travel.state.gov). Check for current Covid entry requirements, such as proof of vaccination or a negative Covid-19 test result.

Arrange your transportation. Book your international flights. Figure out your transportation options. If traveling beyond Venice, research train reservations, rail passes, and car rentals.

Book rooms well in advance, especially if your trip falls during peak season or any major holidays or festivals.

Reserve ahead for key sights. Consider reserving entry slots in advance for St. Mark's Basilica, the Doge's Palace, and the Campanile bell tower.

Consider travel insurance. Compare the cost of insurance to the cost of your potential loss. Check whether your existing insurance (health, homeowners, or renters) covers you and your possessions overseas.

Call your bank. Alert your bank that you'll be using your debit and credit cards in Europe. Ask about transaction fees, and, if you don't already have one, get a "contactless" credit card (request your card PIN, too). You don't need to bring euros; you can withdraw euros from cash machines in Europe.

Use your smartphone smartly. Sign up for an international service plan to reduce your costs, or rely on Wi-Fi instead. Download any apps you'll want on the road, such as maps, translators, transit schedules, and Rick Steves Audio Europe (see sidebar).

Pack light. You'll walk with your luggage more than you think. I travel for weeks with a single carry-on bag and a day pack. Use the packing checklist in Practicalities as a guide.

Travel Smart

If you have a positive attitude, equip yourself with good information (this book), and expect to travel smart, you will.

Pickpockets abound in crowded places where tourists congregate. Treat commotions as smokescreens for theft. Keep your cash,

credit cards, and passport secure in a money belt tucked under your clothes; carry only a day's spending money in your front pocket or wallet.

If you wilt easily, choose a hotel with air-conditioning, start your day early, take a midday siesta, and resume your sightseeing later.

Be sure to schedule in slack time for picnics, laundry, people-watching, leisurely dinners, shopping, and recharging your touristic batteries. Slow down and be open to unexpected experiences and the hospitality of the Italian people.

Stand at a bar and sample some *cicchetti* like a Venetian, sip wine at a canalside restaurant, or dance across a floodlit St. Mark's Square. As you visit places I know and love, I'm happy you'll be meeting some of my favorite Italians.

Happy travels! *Buon viaggio!*

Grand Canal Cruise

Canal Grande

Take a joyride and introduce yourself to Venice by boat. Cruise the Canal Grande on vaporetto line #1 all the way to St. Mark's Square, starting at the train station (Ferrovia) or the bus station (Piazzale Roma).

If it's your first trip down the Grand Canal, you might want to stow this book and just take it all in—Venice is a barrage on the senses that hardly needs narration. On the other hand, these notes give the cruise meaning and help orient you to this great city.

To help you enjoy the visual parade of canal wonders, the tour is keyed to each boat stop. I'll point out both what you can see from the current stop, and what to look forward to as you cruise to the next stop.

Length of This Tour: Allow 45 minutes.

Cost: €9.50 for a 75-minute vaporetto ticket, or covered by a pass—best choice if you want to hop on and off (see page 197).

When to Go: Avoid the morning rush hour (8:00-10:00), when everyone is headed to San Marco. In the evening, sunset bathes the buildings in gold. After dark, chandeliers light up building interiors.

Seating Strategies: You're more likely to find an empty seat if you catch the vaporetto at Piazzale Roma—the stop *before* Ferrovia (a five-minute walk away). With a standard boat and normal crowds, I'd head for the open-air section in the stern and grab the middle seat. Your worst option is sitting inside and trying to look out the window.

Catching Your Boat: This tour is designed to be done on the slow boat #1—any other boat skips too many stops. We'll start at the Ferrovia vaporetto stop (at Santa Lucia train station). In summer, the #1 boat to San Marco generally leaves from dock E (far to the right).

Stops to Consider: You might want to hop on and off along the way. These stops are all worth considering: San Marcuola (Jewish Ghetto), Rialto Mercato (fish market and famous bridge), Ca' Rezzonico (Museum of 18th-Century Venice), Accademia (art museum and the nearby Peggy Guggenheim Collection), and Salute (huge, art-filled church).

Tours: 🎧 Download my free Grand Canal Cruise audio tour.

Starring: Palaces, markets, boats, bridges—Venice.

BACKGROUND

The Grand Canal is Venice's "Main Street." At more than two miles long, nearly 150 feet wide, and nearly 15 feet deep, it's the city's largest canal, lined with its most impressive palaces. It's the remnant of a river that once spilled from the mainland into the Adriatic. The sediment it carried formed barrier islands that cut Venice off from the sea, forming a lagoon.

Venice was built on the marshy islands of the former delta, sitting on wood pilings driven nearly 15 feet into the clay (alder was the preferred wood). About 25 miles of canals drain the city, dumping like streams into the Grand Canal. Technically, Venice has only three canals: Grand, Giudecca, and Cannaregio. The 45 small waterways that dump into the Grand Canal are referred to as rivers (e.g., Rio Novo).

Venice is a city of palaces, dating from the days it was the world's richest city. The most lavish palaces formed a grand architectural cancan along the Grand Canal. Once frescoed in reds and blues, with black-and-white borders and gold-leaf trim, they made Venice a city of dazzling color. This cruise is the only way to truly appreciate the palaces, approaching them at water level, where their main entrances were located. Today, strict laws prohibit any changes in these buildings, so while landowners gnash their teeth, we can enjoy Europe's best-preserved medieval/Renaissance city—slowly rotting. Many of the grand buildings are now vacant. Others harbor chandeliered elegance above mossy, empty (often flooded) ground floors.

Grand Canal

Vaporetto Stops

1. Ferrovia
2. Riva de Biasio
3. San Marcuola
4. San Stae
5. Ca' d'Oro
6. Rialto Mercato
7. Rialto
8. San Silvestro
9. Sant'Angelo
10. San Tomà
11. Ca' Rezzonico
12. Accademia
13. Santa Maria del Giglio
14. Salute
15. San Marco
16. San Zaccaria

Traghetto Stops

A. Traghetto Santa Sofia
B. Traghetto San Tomà
C. Traghetto Santa Maria del Giglio

To
San Michele,
Murano,
Burano &
Torcello

FONDAMENTE NOVE

Lagoon

PALAZZO
MARCELLO

PALAZZO MOLIN

PALAZZO ZULLAN

PALAZZO BARBARIGO

4

CANNAREGIO

SAN
STAE

PALAZZO
FONTANA

PAL.
DONA

STRADA
NOVA

PALAZZO
GIUSTI

PALAZZO
SAGREDO

CA'
'ESARO

CA'
D'ORO

5   **A**

PAL.
FAVRETTO

PALAZZO
MICHIEL COLONNE

PAL.
BRANDO-
LIN

PALAZZO
CORNER
DELLA REGINA

PALAZZO
VALMARANA

FISH
MARKET

6

PALAZZO
CA' DA MOSTO

HOSPITAL

PRODUCE
MARKET

PALAZZO
CIVRAN

SANTI
GIOVANNI E PAOLO
(SAN ZANIPOLO)

POLO

**T FONDACO
DEI TEDESCHI
MALL**

RIALTO
BRIDGE

7

PALAZZO
PAPADOPOLI

PALAZZO
BARZIZZA

PALAZZO
DOLFIN-MANIN

SAL. S. LIO

S. MARIA
FORMOSA

8

PALAZZO
DONA

PALAZZO
BEMBO

MERCERIE

PALAZZO
BERNARDO

PALAZZO
GRIMANI

PALAZZO
FARSETTI-
DANDOLO

CASTELLO

PALAZZO
BENZON

PAL.
CORNER-
CONTARINI

PALAZZO
CORNER-
SPINELLI

PALAZZO
MARTINENGO

FABBRI

MERCERIE

CLOCK
TOWER

ST.
MARK'S
BASILICA

SAN
ZACCARIA

CAMPANILE

SAN
MARCO

DOGE'S
PALACE

BRIDGE
OF SIGHS

SAN MARCO

TOUR ENDS

16 V V **A** V V

CALLE LARGA
XXII MARZO

HARRY'S
AMERICAN
BAR

SAN MARCO &
SAN TEODORO
COLUMNS

To
Lido

CA'
GRANDE

A

GRITTI
PALACE
HOTEL

15

13 **C**

PALAZZO
FLANGINI

Canal

St. Mark's
Basin

PEGGY
GUGGEN.
COLLECTION

PAL.
GENOVESE

14

LA
SALUTE
CHURCH

PUNTA DELLA
DOGANA MUSEUM

To
San Giorgio
Maggiore & Giudecca

200 Meters
200 Yards

THE TOUR BEGINS

❶ Ferrovia

This site has been the gateway into Venice since 1860, when the first train station was built. The **Santa Lucia station,** one of the few modern buildings in town, was built in 1954. The "F.S." logo above the entry stands for "Ferrovie dello Stato," the Italian state railway system.

More than 20,000 people a day commute in from the mainland, making this the busiest part of Venice during rush hour. The nearby **Calatrava Bridge,** spanning the Grand Canal between the train station and Piazzale Roma upstream, was built in 2008 to alleviate some of the congestion.

❷ Riva de Biasio

Venice's main thoroughfare is busy with all kinds of **boats:** taxis, police boats, garbage boats, ambulances, construction cranes, and even brown-and-white UPS boats. Somehow they all manage to share the canal in relative peace.

About 25 yards past the Riva de Biasio stop, look left down the broad Cannaregio Canal to see what was the Jewish Ghetto. The twin, pale pink, six-story "skyscrapers"—the tallest buildings you'll see at this end of the canal—are reminders of how densely populated the world's original ghetto was. This urban island developed into one of the most closely knit business and cultural quarters of all the Jewish communities in Italy, and gave us our word "ghetto" (from *geto,* for the copper foundry once located here).

Ferrovia, a.k.a. Santa Lucia train station

The Grand Canal, lined with grand buildings

❸ San Marcuola

At this stop, facing a tiny square just ahead, stands the unfinished Church of San Marcuola, one of only five churches fronting the Grand Canal. Centuries ago, this canal was a commercial drag of expensive real estate in high demand by wealthy merchants. About 20 yards ahead on the right (across the Grand Canal) stands the stately gray **Turkish Exchange** (Fondaco dei Turchi), one of the oldest houses in Venice. Its horseshoe arches and roofline of triangles and dingle balls are reminders of its Byzantine heritage. Turkish traders in turbans docked here, unloaded their goods into the warehouse on the bottom story, then went upstairs for a home-style meal and a place to sleep. Venice in the 1500s was very cosmopolitan, welcoming every religion and ethnicity, so long as they carried cash. (Today the building contains the city's Museum of Natural History—and Venice's only dinosaur skeleton.)

Just 100 yards ahead on the left (the tallest building with the red canopy), Venice's **Casinò** is housed in the palace where German composer Richard (*The Ring*) Wagner died in 1883. See his distinct, strong-jawed profile in the white plaque on the brick wall. In the 1700s, Venice was Europe's Vegas, with casinos and sex workers everywhere. *Casinòs* ("little houses" in Venetian dialect) have long provided Italians with a handy escape from daily life. Today they're run by the state to keep Mafia influence at bay. Notice the fancy front porch, rolling out the red carpet for high rollers arriving by taxi or hotel boat.

❹ San Stae

The San Stae Church sports a delightful Baroque facade. Opposite the San Stae stop is a little canal opening—on the second building to the

Turkish "Fondaco" Exchange

San Stae Church

right of that opening, look for the peeling plaster that once made up **frescoes** (you can barely distinguish the scant remains of little angels on the lower floors). Imagine the facades of the Grand Canal at their finest. Most of them would have been covered in frescoes by the best artists of the day. As colorful as the city is today, it's still only a faded, sepia-toned remnant of a long-gone era, a time of lavishly decorated, brilliantly colored palaces.

Just ahead (on the right, with blue posts) is the ornate white facade of **Ca' Pesaro** (which houses the International Gallery of Modern Art). *"Ca'"* is short for *casa* (house).

In this city of masks, notice how the rich marble facades along the Grand Canal mask what are generally just simple, no-nonsense brick buildings. Most merchants enjoyed showing off. However, being smart businessmen, they only decorated the sides of the buildings that would be seen and appreciated. But look back as you pass Ca' Pesaro. It's the only building you'll see with a fine side facade. Ahead (about 100 yards on the left) is Ca' d'Oro, with its glorious triple-decker medieval arcade (just before the next stop).

⑤ Ca' d'Oro

The lacy Ca' d'Oro (House of Gold) is the best example of Venetian Gothic architecture on the canal. Although a simple brick construction, its facade is one of the city's finest. Its three stories offer different variations on balcony design, topped with a spiny white roofline. Venetian Gothic mixes traditional Gothic (pointed arches and round medallions stamped with a four-leaf clover) with Byzantine styles (tall, narrow arches atop thin columns), filled in with Islamic frills.

Ca' Pesaro—this *"ca'"* houses modern art   Ca' d'Oro—textbook Venetian Gothic

Traghetto: a short-haul gondola

Rialto Mercato hosts the produce market.

Like all the palaces, this was originally painted and gilded to make it even more glorious than it is now. Today the Ca' d'Oro is an art gallery.

Look at the Venetian chorus line of palaces in front of the boat. On the right is the arcade of the covered **fish market,** with the open-air **produce market** just beyond. This is a great scene to wander through—even though European Union hygiene standards have made it cleaner but less colorful than it once was.

Find the ***traghetto*** gondola ferrying shoppers—standing like Washington crossing the Delaware—back and forth. While once much more numerous, today only three *traghetto* crossings survive along the Grand Canal, each one marked by a classy low-key green-and-black sign. Piloting a *traghetto* isn't the normal day job of these gondoliers. As a public service, all gondoliers are obliged to row a *traghetto* a few days a month. Make a point to use them. At €2 a ride, *traghetti* offer the cheapest gondola ride in Venice (but at this price, don't expect them to sing to you).

❻ Rialto Mercato

This stop serves the busy market. Directly ahead (on the left), is the former trading center for German merchants, built in the 16th century. It's now T Fondaco dei Tedeschi, a luxury shopping mall with great rooftop views. Rising above it is the tip of the Campanile (bell tower), crowned by its golden-angel weathervane at St. Mark's Square, where this tour will end.

You'll cruise by some trendy and beautifully situated wine bars on the right, but look ahead as you round the corner and see the impressive Rialto Bridge come into view.

A major landmark, the **Rialto Bridge** is lined with shops and

Rialto Bridge, with its 160-foot single span, marks Venice's traditional commercial neighborhood.

tourists. Constructed in 1588, it's the third bridge built on this spot. Until the 1850s, this was the only bridge crossing the Grand Canal. With a span of 160 feet and foundations stretching 650 feet on either side, the Rialto was an impressive engineering feat in its day. Earlier bridges here could open to let big ships in, but not this one. By the time it was completed in the 16th century, Venetian trading power was ebbing. After that, much of the Grand Canal was closed to shipping and became a canal of palaces.

When gondoliers pass under the fat arch of the Rialto Bridge, they take full advantage of its acoustics: *"Volare, oh, oh..."*

❼ Rialto

Rialto, a separate town in the early days of Venice, has always been the commercial district, while San Marco was the religious and governmental center. Today, a winding street called the Mercerie connects the two, providing travelers with human traffic jams and a mesmerizing gauntlet of shopping temptations. This is one of the only stretches of the historic Grand Canal with landings upon which you can walk. Boats unloaded the city's basic necessities here: oil, wine, charcoal, iron. Today, the quay is lined with tourist-trap restaurants.

Venice's sleek, black, graceful **gondolas** are a symbol of the city.

With about 500 gondoliers joyriding amid the churning vaporetti, there's a lot of congestion on the Grand Canal. Pay attention—this is where most of the gondola and vaporetto accidents take place. While the Rialto is the highlight of many gondola rides, gondoliers understandably prefer the quieter small canals. Watch your vaporetto driver curse the better-paid gondoliers.

Ahead 100 yards on the left, two gray-colored **palaces** stand side by side (City Hall and the mayor's office). Their horseshoe-shaped, arched windows are similar and their stories are the same height, lining up to create the effect of one long balcony.

❽ San Silvestro

We now enter a long stretch of important **merchants' palaces,** each with proud and different facades. Because ships couldn't navigate beyond the Rialto Bridge, the biggest palaces—with the major shipping needs—line this last stretch of the navigable Grand Canal.

Palaces like these were multifunctional: ground floor for the warehouse, offices and showrooms upstairs, and living quarters above, on the "noble floors" (with big windows to allow in maximum light). Servants lived and worked on the very top floors (with the smallest windows). For fire-safety reasons, kitchens were also located on the top floors. Peek into the noble floors to catch a glimpse of their still-glorious chandeliers of Murano glass.

❾ Sant'Angelo

Notice how many buildings have a foundation of waterproof white stone (*pietra d'Istria*) upon which the bricks sit high and dry. Many canal-level floors are abandoned as the rising water level takes its toll.

Merchant's palace with water-level entries

Docking posts painted the family colors

The **posts**—historically painted gaily with the equivalent of family coats of arms—don't rot underwater. But the wood at the waterline, where it's exposed to oxygen, does. On the smallest canals, little "no motorboats" signs indicate that these canals are for gondolas only (no motorized craft, 5 kph speed limit, no wake).

❿ San Tomà

Fifty yards ahead, on the right side (with twin obelisks on the rooftop), stands **Palazzo Balbi,** the palace of an early-17th-century captain general of the sea. This palace, like so many in the city, flies three flags: Italy (green-white-red), the European Union (blue with ring of stars), and Venice (a lion on a field of red and gold). Today it houses the administrative headquarters of the regional government.

Just past the admiral's palace, look immediately to the right, down a side canal. On the right side of that canal, before the bridge, see the traffic light and the **fire station** (the 1930s Mussolini-era building with four arches hiding fireboats parked and ready to go).

The impressive **Ca' Foscari,** with a classic Venetian facade (on the corner, across from the fire station), dominates the bend in the canal. This is the main building of the University of Venice, which has about 25,000 students.

The grand, heavy, white **Ca' Rezzonico,** just before the stop of the same name, houses the Museum of 18th-Century Venice. Across the canal is the cleaner and leaner **Palazzo Grassi,** the last major palace built on the canal, erected in the late 1700s. It was purchased by a French tycoon and now displays part of Punta della Dogana's contemporary art collection.

Ca' Foscari, now part of the university

Ca' Rezzonico evokes 18th-century luxury.

Accademia Bridge—great viewpoint and gateway to the art-filled Dorsoduro neighborhood

⓫ Ca' Rezzonico

Up ahead, the Accademia Bridge leads over the Grand Canal to the **Accademia Gallery** (right side), filled with the best Venetian paintings. There was no bridge here until 1854, when a cast-iron one was built. It was replaced with this wooden bridge in 1933. While meant to be temporary, it still stands today, nearly a century later.

⓬ Accademia

From here, look through the graceful bridge and way ahead to enjoy a classic view of **La Salute Church,** topped by a crown-shaped dome supported by scrolls. This Church of St. Mary of Good Health was built to ask God to deliver Venetians from the devastating plague of 1630 (which had killed about a third of the city's population).

The low, white building among greenery (100 yards ahead, on the right, between the Accademia Bridge and the church) is the **Peggy Guggenheim Collection.** The American heiress and art patron relocated here after World War II, sprucing up a palace that had been abandoned in mid-construction. Peggy willed the city her fine collection of modern art.

Two doors past the Guggenheim, Palazzo Dario has a great set of characteristic **funnel-shaped chimneys.** These forced embers through a loop-the-loop channel until they were dead—required in the days when stone palaces were surrounded by humble wooden buildings, and a live spark could make a merchant's workforce homeless. Notice this early Renaissance building's flat-feeling facade with "pasted-on" Renaissance motifs. Three doors later is the **Salviati building,** which once served as a glassworks. Its fine Art Nouveau mosaic, done in the early 20th century, features Venice as a queen being appreciated by the big shots of society.

⓭ Santa Maria del Giglio

Back on the left stands the fancy Gritti Palace hotel. Hemingway and Woody Allen both stayed here.

Take a deep whiff of Venice. What's all this nonsense about stinky canals? All I smell is my shirt. By the way, how's your captain? Smooth dockings?

⓮ Salute

The huge La Salute Church towers overhead as if squirted from a can of Catholic Reddi-wip. Like Venice itself, the church rests upon pilings. To build the foundation for the city, thousands of trees were piled together, reaching beneath the mud to the solid clay.

As the Grand Canal opens up into the lagoon, the last building on the right with the golden ball is the 17th-century **Customs House,** which now houses the Punta della Dogana contemporary art museum. Its two bronze Atlases hold a statue of Fortune riding the ball. Arriving ships stopped here to pay their tolls.

⓯ San Marco

Up ahead on the left, the green pointed tip of the Campanile marks **St. Mark's Square,** the political and religious center of Venice...and the final destination of this tour. You could get off at the San Marco stop and go straight to St. Mark's Square. But I'm staying on the boat for one more stop, just past St. Mark's Square (it's a quick walk back).

Survey the lagoon. Opposite St. Mark's Square, across the water, the ghostly white church with the pointy bell tower is **San Giorgio Maggiore,** with great views of Venice. Next to it is the residential island Giudecca, stretching from close to San Giorgio Maggiore past the Venice youth hostel (with a nice view, directly across) to the Hilton Hotel (good nighttime view, far right end of island).

La Salute Church—its towering dome is topped with a statue of "Our Lady of Health."

Still on board? If you are, as we leave the San Marco stop look left and prepare for a drive-by view of St. Mark's Square. First comes the bold, white facade of the old mint (in front of the bell tower) marked by a tiny cupola yet as sturdy as Fort Knox, where Venice's golden ducat, the "dollar" of the Venetian Republic, was made. Next door is the library, its facade just three windows wide. Then comes the city's ceremonial front door: twin columns topped by St. Theodore standing on a crocodile and the winged lion of St. Mark, who've welcomed visitors since the 15th century. Between the columns, catch a glimpse of two giant figures atop the **Clock Tower**—they've been whacking their clappers every hour since 1499. The domes of **St. Mark's Basilica** are soon eclipsed by the lacy facade of the **Doge's Palace.** Next you'll see many gondolas with their green breakwater buoys, the **Bridge of Sighs** (leading from the palace to the prison—check out the maximum-security bars), and finally the grand harborside promenade—the **Riva.**

Follow the Riva with your eye, past elegant hotels to the green area in the distance. This is the largest of Venice's few **parks,** which hosts the international Biennale art exhibit. Much farther in the distance is the **Lido,** the island with Venice's beaches. Its sand and casinos are tempting, though given its car traffic, it lacks the medieval charm of Venice.

⑯ San Zaccaria

OK, you're at your last stop. Quick—muscle your way off this boat! (If you don't, you'll eventually end up at the Lido.)

At San Zaccaria, you're right in the thick of the action. A number of other vaporetti depart from here (see page 197). Otherwise, it's a short walk back along the Riva to St. Mark's Square. Ahoy!

St. Mark's Square Tour

Piazza San Marco

Venice was once Europe's richest city, and Piazza San Marco was its center. As middleman in the trade between Asia and Europe, wealthy Venice profited from both sides. In 1450, at its peak, Venice had 150,000 citizens and a gross "national" product that exceeded that of entire countries.

The rich Venetians taught the rest of Europe about the good life—silks, spices, and jewels from the East, crafts from northern Europe, good food and wine, fine architecture, music, theater, and laughter. Venice was a vibrant city full of painted palaces, glittering canals, and impressed visitors. Five centuries after its power began to decline, Venice still has all of these things, with the added charm of romantic decay. In this tour, we'll spend an hour in the heart of this Old World superpower.

ORIENTATION

Getting There: Signs all over town point to *San Marco,* located where the Grand Canal spills out into the lagoon. Vaporetto stops: San Marco or San Zaccaria.

Campanile: €10 on-site; €12 timed-entry ticket lets you skip the line (buy online in advance or use the posted QR code at the entrance to book on the spot); daily roughly 9:30-20:45, shorter hours off-season; may close during bad weather.

Clock Tower: To see the interior, you need to book a spot on a tour (see page 131).

Tours: 🎧 Download my free St. Mark's Square **audio tour.**

Services: Pay WCs are behind the Correr Museum and also at the waterfront park, Giardinetti Reali (near San Marco-Vallaresso vaporetto dock).

Eating: Cafés with live music provide an engaging soundtrack for St. Mark's Square (see the "Cafés on St. Mark's Square" sidebar, later). The Correr Museum (at the end of the square opposite the basilica) has a quiet upstairs coffee shop overlooking the crowded square. For a list of restaurants in the area, see page 179.

Starring: Byzantine domes, Gothic arches, Renaissance arches...and the wonderful, musical space they enclose.

Mark's winged lion appears everywhere.

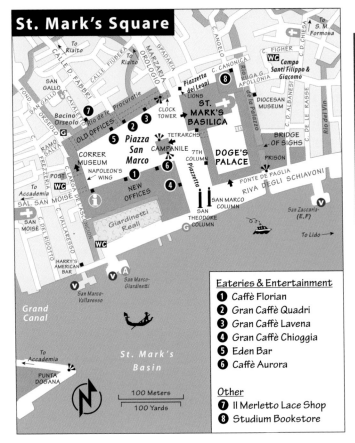

St. Mark's Square

Eateries & Entertainment
1 Caffè Florian
2 Gran Caffè Quadri
3 Gran Caffè Lavena
4 Gran Caffè Chioggia
5 Eden Bar
6 Caffè Aurora

Other
7 Il Merletto Lace Shop
8 Studium Bookstore

THE TOUR BEGINS

▶ *For an overview of this grand square and the buildings that surround it, view it from the west end of the square (away from St. Mark's Basilica).*

The Piazza

St. Mark's Basilica dominates the square with its Eastern-style onion domes and glowing mosaics. Mark Twain said it looked like "a vast warty bug taking a meditative walk." (I say it looks like tiara-wearing ladybugs copulating.) To the right of the basilica is its 325-foot-tall Campanile. Behind the Campanile you can catch a glimpse of the pale pink Doge's Palace. Lining the square are the former government offices (*procuratie*) that administered the Venetian empire's vast network of trading outposts, which stretched all the way to Turkey.

The square is big, but it feels intimate with its cafés and dueling orchestras. By day, it's great for people-watching and pigeon-chasing. By night, under lantern light, it transports you to another century, complete with its own romantic soundtrack.

For architecture buffs, here are three centuries of styles, bam, side by side, *uno-due-tre,* for easy comparison:

1. On the left (as you face the basilica) are the "old" offices, built about 1500 in solid, column-and-arch Renaissance style. Closed to the public for 500 years, the offices are being restored to host art exhibitions, installations, and seminars (may be open by the time you visit).

2. The "new" offices (on the right), in a High Renaissance style from a century later (c. 1600), are a little heavier and more ornate. This wing mixes arches and the three orders of columns in layers from bottom to top—Doric, Ionic, and Corinthian.

3. Napoleon's wing, at the end opposite from the basilica, is later and designed to fit in. The dozen Roman emperors decorating the parapet were once joined by Napoleon in the middle, but today the French emperor is gone. The Correr Museum is housed in this wing.

The arcade ringing the square provides an elegant promenade—complete with drapes to provide relief from the sun.

Imagine this square full of water. That happens every so often at very high tides (*acqua alta*), a reminder that Venice and the sea are intertwined. (Now, as one sinks and the other rises, they are more intertwined than ever.)

Venice became Europe's richest city from its trade with northern Europeans, Ottoman Muslims, and Byzantine Christians. Here in St. Mark's Square, the exact center of this East-West axis, we see the luxury and cosmopolitan mix of East and West.

Watch out for pigeon speckle. Venetians don't like pigeons, but they do like seagulls—because they eat pigeons. In 2008, Venice outlawed the feeding of pigeons. But tourists—eager for a pigeon-clad photo op—haven't gotten that message.

▶ *Now approach the basilica. If it's hot and you're tired, grab a shady spot at the foot of the Campanile.*

St. Mark's Basilica

The facade is a wild mix of East and West, with round, Roman-style arches over the doorways, golden Byzantine mosaics, a roofline ringed with pointed Gothic pinnacles, and topped with Muslim-style onion domes (made of wood, covered with lead). The brick-structure building is blanketed in marble that came from Constantinople (in 1204), which originally had looted the materials from throughout the eastern

The piazza is magnificent whether floodlit or flooded—as it occasionally is at *acqua alta*.

Cafés on St. Mark's Square

In Venice's heyday, it was said that the freedoms a gentleman could experience here went far beyond what any true gentleman would actually care to indulge in. But one extravagance all could enjoy was the ritual of publicly consuming coffee: showing off with an affordable luxury, while sharing the ideas of the Enlightenment.

Exotic coffee was made to order for the fancy café scene. Traders introduced coffee, called the "wine of Islam," from the Middle East. The first coffeehouses opened in the 17th century, and by 1750 there were dozens of cafés lining Piazza San Marco and 200 operating in Venice.

Today, several fine old cafés survive and still line the square. Those with live music feature similar food, prices, and a three- to five-piece combo playing a selection of classical and pop hits, from Brahms to "Bésame Mucho."

You can wander around the square listening to the different orchestras, or take a seat at a café. At any place with live music, it's perfectly acceptable to nurse a cappuccino for an hour—you're paying for the music with the cover charge. Or you can sip your coffee at the bar at a nearly normal price. If you sit outside and get just an espresso (your cheapest option), expect to pay €12.50—€6.50 for the coffee and a €6 cover charge when the orchestra is playing (most of the day). Service is included (no need to tip).

Caffè Florian (on the right as you face the church) is the most famous and was one of the first places in Europe to serve coffee. It's

Mediterranean. There are columns from Alexandria, capitals from Sicily, and carvings from Anatolia. The columns flanking the doorways show the facade's variety—purple, green, gray, white, yellow, some speckled, some striped horizontally, some vertically, some fluted—all topped with a variety of different capitals.

What's amazing isn't so much the variety as the fact that the whole thing comes together in a bizarre sort of harmony. St. Mark's is simply the most interesting church in Europe, a church that (to paraphrase Goethe) "can only be compared with itself."

For more on the basilica, inside and out, see the 📖 St. Mark's Basilica Tour chapter.

▶ *Facing the basilica, turn 90 degrees to the left to see the...*

been a popular spot for a discreet rendezvous in Venice since 1720. The orchestra plays a more classical repertoire compared with others on the square. Though the main action is outside, do walk inside through the richly decorated, old-time rooms where Casanova, Charles Dickens, and Woody Allen have all paid too much for a drink.

Gran Caffè Quadri, opposite the Florian and established in 1780, has another illustrious roster of famous clientele.

Gran Caffè Lavena, near the Clock Tower, is less storied—although it dates from 1750 and counts composer Richard Wagner as a former regular. Drop in to check out its dazzling but politically incorrect chandelier.

Gran Caffè Chioggia, on the Piazzetta facing the Doge's Palace, charges no cover and has one or two musicians playing—usually a pianist.

Eden Bar and **Caffè Aurora** are less expensive and don't have live music.

Clock Tower (Torre dell'Orologio)

Any proper Renaissance city wanted to have a prominent gate with a clock tower as its formal entrance. In Venice's case, its entry was visible from the sea. The Clock Tower retains some of its original blue and gold pigments, a reminder that, in centuries past, this city glowed with bright color.

Two bronze "Moors" stand atop the Clock Tower. Built originally to be Caucasian giants, they only switched ethnicity when their metal darkened over the centuries. At the top of each hour they swing their giant clappers. The clock dial shows the 24 hours, the signs of the zodiac, and in the blue center, the phases of the moon—practical information, as a maritime city with a shallow lagoon needs to know the

The Basilica's Byzantine-flavored domes

The Clock Tower's statues chime the hours.

tides. Above the dial is the world's first digital clock, which changes every five minutes.

An alert winged lion, the symbol of St. Mark and the city, looks down on the crowded square. He opens a book that reads *"Pax Tibi Marce,"* or "Peace to you, Mark." As legend goes, these were the comforting words that an angel spoke to the stressed evangelist, assuring him he would find serenity during a stormy night that the saint spent here on the island. Eventually, St. Mark's body found its final resting place inside the basilica, and now his winged-lion symbol is everywhere. (Find four in 20 seconds. Go.)

Venice's many lions express the city's various mood swings through history—triumphant after a naval victory, sad when a favorite son has died, hollow-eyed after a plague, and smiling when the soccer team wins. Every Venetian child born since the dawn of cameras has probably been photographed riding one of the pair of lions squatting between the Clock Tower and the basilica.

Campanile

The original Campanile (bell tower) was an observation tower and a marvel of medieval and Renaissance architecture until 1902, when it toppled into the center of the piazza. It had groaned ominously the night before, sending people scurrying from the cafés. The next morning...*crash!* The golden angel on top landed right at the basilica's front door, standing up.

The Campanile was rebuilt 10 years later complete with its golden archangel Gabriel, who always faces the breeze. You can ride an elevator to the top for one of the best views of Venice (though it can be crowded at peak times).

Because St. Mark's Square is the first place in town to start flooding, there are tide gauges at the outside base of the Campanile (near the exit, facing the square) that show the current sea level (*livello marea*). Find the stone plaque (near the exit door) that commemorates the high-water 77-inch level from the disastrous floods of 1966. In November 2019, Venice suffered another terrible high tide, cresting at 60 inches.

If the tide is mild (around 20 inches), the water merely seeps up through the drains. But when there's a strong tide (around 40 inches), the water bubbles upward and flows like a river to the lowest points in the square, which can be covered with a few inches of water in an hour or so. When the water level rises one meter above mean sea level, a warning siren sounds, and it repeats if a serious flood is imminent.

Many doorways have three-foot-high wooden or metal barriers to block the high water, but the seawater still seeps in through floors and drains, rendering the barriers nearly useless.

You might see stacked wooden benches in the square; during floods, the benches are placed end-to-end to create elevated sidewalks. If you think the square is crowded now, when it's flooded it turns into total gridlock, as all the people normally sharing the whole square jostle for space on the narrow, raised wooden walkways.

In 2006, the pavement around St. Mark's Square was taken up, and the entire height of the square was raised by adding a layer of sand and then replacing the stones. If the columns along the ground floor of the Doge's Palace look stubby, it's because this process has been carried out many times over the centuries, buying a little more time as the sea slowly swallows the city.

▶ *The small square between the basilica and the water is the...*

Many generations have struck the same pose.

The Basilica's bell tower, or Campanile

Piazzetta

This "Little Square" is framed by the Doge's Palace on the left, the library on the right, and the waterfront of the lagoon. In former days, the Piazzetta was closed to the public for a few hours a day so that government officials and bigwigs could gather in the sun to strike shady deals.

The pale pink **Doge's Palace** is the epitome of the style known as Venetian Gothic. Columns support traditional, pointed Gothic arches, but with a Venetian flair—they're curved to a point, ornamented with a trefoil (three-leaf clover), and topped with a round medallion of a quatrefoil (four-leaf clover). The pattern is found on buildings all over Venice and on the formerly Venetian-controlled Croatian coast, but nowhere else in the world (except Las Vegas).

The two large 12th-century **columns** near the water were (like so much else) looted from Constantinople. Mark's winged lion sits on top of one. The lion's body (nearly 15 feet long) predates the wings and is more than 2,000 years old. The other column holds St. Theodore (battling a crocodile), the former patron saint who was replaced by Mark. I guess stabbing crocs in the back isn't classy enough for an upwardly mobile world power. After public ridicule, criminals were executed by being hung from these columns in the hope that the public could learn its lessons vicariously.

Venice was the "Bride of the Sea" because she depended on sea trading for her livelihood. This "marriage" was celebrated annually by the people on Ascension Day. The doge, in full regalia, boarded a ritual boat here at the edge of the Piazzetta and sailed out into the lagoon. There a vow was made, and he dropped a jeweled ring into the water to seal the marriage.

The Piazzetta and the Doge's Palace

Venetian Gothic—arches and medallions

In the distance, on an island across the lagoon, is one of the grandest views in the city, of the Church of San Giorgio Maggiore. With its four tall columns as the entryway, the church, designed by the late-Renaissance architect Andrea Palladio, influenced the appearance of future government and bank buildings around the world.

Palladio's sober classical lines are pure and intellectual, but with their love of extravagance, Venetians wanted something more exuberant. More to local taste was the High Renaissance style of Jacopo Sansovino, who (around 1530) designed the library (here on the Piazzetta) and the delicate Loggetta at the base of the Campanile (destroyed by the collapse of the tower in 1902 and then pieced back together).

Tetrarchs and the Doge's Palace's Seventh Column

Where the basilica meets the Doge's Palace is the traditional entrance to the palace, decorated with an ancient Roman statue of the four **Tetrarchs.** This dates from the fourth century AD, after Rome was divided into two empires. It features the emperors of the east and west (bearded and wise), each with their younger (and not bearded) successors. It serves as a decorative cornerstone of a tower from the doges' fortress (which was destroyed in 976). I like to think they're the scared leaders of a divided Rome during its fall, holding their swords and each other as all hell breaks loose around them. These statues—made of precious purple porphyry stone (quarried in Egypt)—are symbols of power. They were looted from Constantinople (1204), and then placed here proudly as spoils of war.

Nearby is more booty from the Crusades. The two square pillars to the left decorated a Genovese fortress in Palestine that was taken by

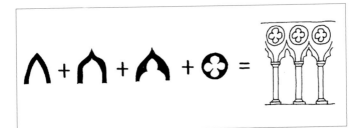

Escape from St. Mark's Square

Crowds getting to you? Here are some relatively quiet areas on or near St. Mark's Square.

Correr Museum Café: Sip a cappuccino in the café of this uncrowded history museum that overlooks St. Mark's Square (entrance at far end of the piazza, no museum ticket necessary). See page 128.

Giardinetti Reali: This small park along the waterfront is the only place near the square for a legal picnic (it's west of the Piazzetta—facing the water, turn right).

Il Merletto: This lace shop is in a small, decommissioned chapel near the northwest corner of St. Mark's Square (go through Sotoportego del Cavalletto and across the little bridge on the right).

La Salute Church: This cool church in a quiet neighborhood is a short hop on vaporetto #1 from the San Marco-Vallaresso stop. See page 139.

Caffè Florian: The plush interior of this luxurious 18th-century café on St. Mark's Square is generally quiet and nearly empty. A coffee here can be a wonderful break (see the "Cafés on St. Mark's Square" sidebar, earlier).

the Venetians in the 13th century. And just beyond that, at the corner of the basilica, is a purple four-foot-tall column—a pedestal for the official government herald announcing decrees, laws, and news...more loot from Constantinople.

About two-thirds of the way down the Doge's Palace, look for a **column** that's slightly shorter and fatter than the rest (it's the seventh from the water). Its carved capital tells a story of love, romance, and tragedy: 1) In the first scene (the carving facing the Piazzetta), a woman on a balcony is wooed by her lover, who says, "Babe, I want *you!*" 2) She responds, "Why, little ol' *me?*" 3) They get married. 4) Kiss. 5) Hit the sack—pretty racy for 14th-century art. 6) Nine months later, guess what? 7) The baby takes its first steps. 8) And as was all too common in the 1300s...the child dies.

▶ *Continue down the Piazzetta to the waterfront. Turn left and walk (east) along the water. At the top of the first bridge, look inland at the...*

Bridge of Sighs

In the Doge's Palace (on your left), the government doled out justice. On your right are the prisons. (Don't let the palatial facade fool you—see the bars on the windows?) Prisoners sentenced in the palace

The Bridge of Sighs connects the rich Doge's Palace (left) with its notorious prisons (right).

crossed to the prisons by way of the covered bridge in front of you. This was called the Prisons' Bridge until the Romantic poet Lord Byron renamed it in the 19th century. From this bridge, the convicted got their final view of sunny, joyous Venice before entering the black and dank prisons. According to the Romantic legend, they sighed.

Venice has been a major tourist center for four centuries. Anyone who's ever come here has stood on this very spot, looking at the Bridge of Sighs. Lean on the railing leaned on by everyone from Casanova to Byron to Hemingway.

> *I stood in Venice, on the Bridge of Sighs;*
> *A palace and a prison on each hand:*
> *I saw from out the wave, her structures rise*
> *As from the stroke of the enchanter's wand:*
> *A thousand years their cloudy wings expand*
> *Around me, and a dying glory smiles*
> *O'er the far times when many a subject land*
> *Looked to the winged Lion's marble piles,*
> *Where Venice sat in state, throned on her hundred isles!*
> —Lord Byron, *Childe Harold's Pilgrimage,* Canto 4

St. Mark's Basilica Tour

Basilica di San Marco

Among Europe's churches, St. Mark's is peerless. From the outside, it's a riot of domes, columns, and statues, completely unlike the towering Gothic churches of northern Europe or the heavy Baroque of much of the rest of Italy. Inside is a decor of mosaics, colored marbles, and Byzantine treasures that's rarely seen elsewhere. The Christian symbolism is unfamiliar to Western eyes, done in the style of Byzantine icons and even Islamic designs. Older than most of Europe's churches, it feels like a remnant of a lost world. To truly say you've "seen" the basilica, plan to visit three paid-admission sights within it, which give an up-close look at the church's treasures. This is your best chance in Italy (outside of Ravenna) to glimpse a forgotten and somewhat mysterious part of the human story—Byzantium.

Cost: General admission-€3, timed-entry ticket-€6. Once inside, you can add on any of three separate exhibits within the church (or buy ahead online): Treasury-€5, Golden Altarpiece-€5, and San Marco Museum-€7.

Hours: Mon-Sat 9:30-17:00, Sun 14:00-17:00 (Sun until 16:30 Nov-Easter).

Information: +39 041 270 8311, www.basilicasanmarco.it.

Reservations Recommended: The easiest way to avoid long lines is to reserve an entry time in advance, which lets you bypass the general admission line for a separate entrance. If you're visiting during busy times, book ahead by several days at least.

If you arrive without a reservation, you can head to the "line-skipping" entrance and scan the posted QR code. If there are time slots available—either immediately or for later that day—you can buy a ticket on your mobile phone. For shorter lines and fewer crowds in general, visit early or late.

Dress Code: Modest dress (no bare knees or bare shoulders) is strictly enforced for men, women, and even kids.

Prayers and Church Services: Worshippers may enter the church daily 8:00-19:30 using the Porta dei Fiori door on the north (left) side (Mass times are listed on the basilica website).

Photographers, Take Note: The interior is brilliantly lit Mon-Sat 11:30-12:45. After that, many of the mosaics are in shadow.

Tours: Free hour-long **English tours** (heavy on the mosaics' religious symbolism) may be offered, typically at 11:00 (check website for current schedule). **Audioguides** (€5) are on sale as you enter, or ∩ download my free St. Mark's Basilica **audio tour.**

Length of This Tour: Allow one hour.

Baggage Check: The church will not let you in with a bag. On the north (left) side of the church, you'll find automated storage lockers (€3).

Visitor Services: A WC is inside the San Marco Museum.

Starring: St. Mark, Byzantium, mosaics, and ancient bronze horses.

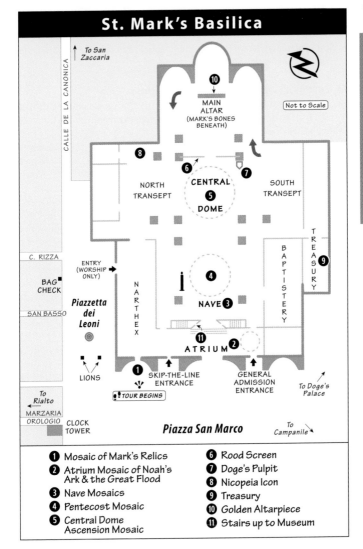

St. Mark's Basilica

To San Zaccaria

CALLE DE LA CANONICA

Not to Scale

10 MAIN ALTAR (MARK'S BONES BENEATH)

8 NICOPEIA ICON

6 ROOD SCREEN

7 DOGE'S PULPIT

NORTH TRANSEPT

5 CENTRAL DOME

SOUTH TRANSEPT

C. RIZZA

BAG CHECK

SAN BASSO

ENTRY (WORSHIP ONLY)

Piazzetta dei Leoni

NARTHEX

4 NAVE **3**

TREASURY **9**

BAPTISTERY

To Rialto

MARZARIA

OROLOGIO

CLOCK TOWER

LIONS

11 STAIRS

2 ATRIUM

SKIP-THE-LINE ENTRANCE

GENERAL ADMISSION ENTRANCE

To Doge's Palace

! TOUR BEGINS

1 MOSAIC OF MARK'S RELICS

Piazza San Marco

To Campanile

1 Mosaic of Mark's Relics
2 Atrium Mosaic of Noah's Ark & the Great Flood
3 Nave Mosaics
4 Pentecost Mosaic
5 Central Dome Ascension Mosaic
6 Rood Screen
7 Doge's Pulpit
8 Nicopeia Icon
9 Treasury
10 Golden Altarpiece
11 Stairs up to Museum

▶ *Start outside in the square, far enough back to take in the whole facade. Then zero in on the details.*

❶ Exterior: Mosaic of Mark's Relics

St. Mark's Basilica is a treasure chest of booty that was looted during Venice's glory days. That's most appropriate for a church built on the stolen bones of a saint.

The **mosaic over the far left door** shows the theft that put Venice on the pilgrimage map. Two men (in the center, with crooked staffs) enter the church bearing a coffin with the body of St. Mark, who looks pretty grumpy from the long voyage.

St. Mark was the author of one of the Gospels, the four Bible books (Matthew, Mark, Luke, and John) telling the story of Jesus' life. Eight centuries after Mark's death, his holy body was in Muslim-occupied Alexandria, Egypt. In AD 829, two visiting Venetian merchants "rescued" the body from the "infidels" and spirited it away to Venice.

The merchants presented the body—not to a pope or bishop, but to the doge (with white ermine collar, on the right) and his wife, the dogaressa (with entourage, on the left), giving instant status to Venice's budding secular state. They built a church here over Mark's bones and made him the patron saint of the city. You'll see his symbol, the winged lion, all over Venice.

The original church burned down in AD 976. Today's structure was begun in 1063. The mosaic, from 1260, shows that the church hasn't changed much since then—you can see the onion domes and famous bronze horses on the balcony.

St. Mark's—a church unlike any other

Mark's body is carried into the church.

The St. Mark's you see today, mostly from the 11th century, was modeled after a great fourth-century church in Constantinople/ Istanbul (the long-gone Church of the Holy Apostles), giving the city deep (if faux) roots.

In subsequent centuries, the church was encrusted with materials looted from buildings throughout the Venetian empire. The facade was decorated with a mishmash of plundered columns. The main entrance is a sixth-century, bronze-paneled Byzantine door that likely swung in Constantinople's Hagia Sophia church. Their prize booty was the four bronze horses that adorn the balcony, stolen from Constantinople during the Fourth Crusade. (These are copies; the originals are inside the church museum.) The atrium you're about to enter was added to serve as their pedestal. No wonder the architectural style of St. Mark's has been called "Early Ransack."

▶ *Enter the atrium of the basilica and find a place to view its ceiling mosaics. (Note that, depending on where the current entrance and exit are, you may have a better chance to study these fine atrium mosaics on your way out.) Start by finding a golden arch overhead with scenes of Noah's Ark.*

❷ Atrium Mosaic of Noah's Ark and the Great Flood

Of all the famous mosaics of St. Mark's, this Flood scene is one of the oldest (13th century), finest, and most accessible.

The scenes show Noah and his sons sawing logs to build the Ark. Venetians—who were great ship builders—could relate. At its peak, Venice's Arsenale warship-building plant employed several thousand workers.

Below that are scenes of Noah putting all species of animals into

Atrium mosaic—Noah's sons saw logs.

After the Flood, Noah releases a dove.

Christ as Pantocrator

Most Eastern Orthodox churches—whose roots lay in the Greek Byzantine world—have at least one mosaic or painting of Christ in a standard pose: as "Pantocrator," a Greek word meaning "Ruler of All." St. Mark's features several images of Christ as Pantocrator (for example, over the altar, in the central dome, and over the entrance door). The image, so familiar to Orthodox Christians, may be a bit foreign to Protestants, Catholics, and secularists.

As King of the Universe, Christ sits (usually on a throne) facing directly out, with penetrating eyes. He wears a halo divided with a cross. In his left hand is a Bible, while his right hand blesses, with the fingers forming the Greek letters *chi* and *rho*, the first two letters of "Christos." The thumb touches the fingers, symbolizing how Christ unites both his divinity and his humanity. On either side of Christ's head are the Greek letters "IC XC," short for "IesuC XristoC."

the Ark, two by two. (Who's at the head of the line? Lions.) Then the Flood hits in full force, drowning the wicked. Noah sends out a dove twice to see whether there's any dry land where he can dock. He finds it, leaves the Ark with a gorgeous rainbow overhead, and offers a sacrifice of thanks to God.

▶ *Rejoin the slow flow of people. Climb a few steps into the church. Just inside the door, step out of the flow and survey the church.*

❸ The Nave: Mosaics Above and Below

As your eyes adjust to the dark, notice that the entire upper part of the church is decorated in mosaic—nearly 5,000 square yards (imagine paving a football field with contact lenses). These golden mosaics are in the Byzantine style, though many were designed by artists from the Italian Renaissance and later. The often-overlooked lower walls are covered with green-, yellow-, purple-, and rose-colored marble slabs, cut to expose the grain, and laid out in geometric patterns. Even the floor is mosaic, with mostly geometrical designs. It rolls like the sea. Venice is sinking and shifting, creating these cresting waves of stone.

Those familiar with Eastern Orthodox churches will find familiar elements in St. Mark's: a central floor plan, domes, mosaics, and iconic images of Mary and Christ as Pantocrator—ruler of all things.

The nave—golden mosaics (on the ceiling), rood screen (midway down), and altar (far end)

Mosaics

St. Mark's mosaics are pictures made by pressing small tiles of colored stone or glass (called *tesserae*) into wet plaster. Ancient Romans paved floors, walls, and ceilings with them. When Rome "fell," the art form died out in the West but was carried on by Byzantine craftsmen. They perfected the gold background effect by

sandwiching pieces of gold leaf between glass. The surfaces of the tiles are purposely cut unevenly to capture light and give off a shimmering effect. The reflecting gold mosaics helped to light thick-walled, small-windowed, lantern-lit Byzantine churches, creating a golden glow that symbolized the divine light of heaven.

St. Mark's mosaics tell the entire Christian history from end to beginning—from the Apocalypse near the entrance to Christ's Old Testament origins near the altar. At either end are images of Christ—the beginning and the end, the Alpha and Omega of the Christian universe.

As your eyes adjust, the mosaics start to give off a mystical, golden luminosity, the atmosphere of the Byzantine heaven. The air itself seems almost visible, like a cloud of incense. It's a subtle effect, one that grows as the filtered light changes. There are more beautiful, bigger, overwhelming, and even holier churches, but none is as stately.

▶ *Find the chandelier in the nave (in the shape of a cathedral space station) and run your eyes up the support chain to the dome above. This has one of the church's greatest mosaics.*

❹ Pentecost Mosaic

In a golden heaven, the dove of the Holy Spirit shoots out a pinwheel of spiritual lasers, igniting tongues of fire on the heads of the 12 apostles below, giving them the ability to speak other languages without a Rick Steves phrase book. You'd think they'd be amazed, but their expressions are as solemn as...icons. One of the oldest mosaics in the church

Ascension Mosaic—12 Apostles and Mary ring the dome beneath Christ in heaven.

(c. 1125), it has distinct "Byzantine" features: a gold background and apostles with halos, solemn faces, almond eyes, delicate blessing hands, and rumpled robes, all facing forward.

This is art from a society still touchy about the Bible's commandment against making "graven images" of holy things. The Byzantine style emphasizes otherworldliness rather than literal human detail.

▶ *Shuffle along with the crowds up to the center of the church.*

❺ Central Dome Ascension Mosaic

Notice the layout: the church has four equal arms, each topped with a dome, radiating out to form a Greek cross (+). The symmetrical floor plan symbolizes perfection, rather than the more common Latin cross of the Crucifixion (emphasizing man's sinfulness).

Now gape upward into the central dome, the very heart of the church. Christ—having lived his miraculous life and having been crucified for man's sins—ascends into the starry sky on a rainbow. He raises his right hand and blesses the universe. This isn't the crucified, mortal Jesus featured in most churches, but a powerful, resurrected God, the ruler of all.

Christ's blessing radiates, rippling down to the ring of

Byzantium, the Fourth Crusade, and Venice

The Byzantine Empire was the eastern half of the ancient Roman Empire that *didn't* "fall" in AD 476. It remained Christian, Greek-speaking, and enlightened for another thousand years.

In AD 330, Constantine, the first Christian emperor, moved the Roman Empire's capital to the newly expanded city of Byzantium, which he humbly renamed Constantinople. Venice had strong ties with Byzantium from its earliest days. Venetian merchants were granted trading rights to Byzantine ports in the Adriatic and eastern Mediterranean. They traded raw materials from Western Europe for luxury goods from the East. As Venice grew more powerful, they wanted still more access to Byzantium's wealth. In the year 1204, they saw their chance. They joined the pope's Crusade to "save" the Holy Land from Muslim influence. But along the way, the ships diverted to Constantinople. The doge-led Crusaders sacked the Byzantine capital and brought the booty home to Venice. In St. Mark's Basilica, you can see these treasures: the bronze horses, bronze doors of Hagia Sophia, Golden Altarpiece enamels, the Treasury's treasures, the Nicopeia icon, and much of the marble that now covers the (brick) church.

Byzantine Empire

Venice
Genoa
Pisa
Rome
Ravenna
Constantinople
Nicaea
Athens
Antioch
Jerusalem

= Empire 1025

white-robed apostles below. Mary is with them, wearing blue with golden Greek crosses on each shoulder and looking ready to play patty-cake. From these saints goodness descends, creating the Virtues and Beatitudes that ring the base of the dome between the windows. In Byzantine churches, the window-lit dome represented heaven, while the dark church below represented earth—a microcosm of the hierarchical universe.

Beneath the dome at the four corners, the four Gospel writers ("Matev," "Marc," "Luca," and "Ioh") thoughtfully scribble down the heavenly events. This wisdom flows down as water pouring from jugs, symbolizing the four great rivers below them, spreading through the church's four equal arms (the "four corners" of the world), and baptizing the congregation with God's love. The church building is a series of perfect circles within perfect squares—the cosmic order—with Christ in the center solemnly blessing us. God's in his heaven, saints are on earth, and all's right with the world.

The Church as Theater

Look around at the church's furnishings and imagine a service here. The ❻ **rood screen** (like the iconostasis in a Greek church), topped with 14 saints, separates the congregation from the high altar, heightening the "mystery" of the Mass. The ❼ **pulpit** (the purple one on the right) was reserved for the doge, who led prayers and made important announcements.

Even today, the Venetian church service is a theatrical multimedia spectacle, combining words (prayers, Bible readings in Latin and Greek), music (chants, choir, organ, musicians), set design (mosaics, rood screen), costumes and props (robes, reliquaries, candles, incense), and even stage direction (processionals through the crowd). Coincidentally or not, the first modern opera—also a multimedia theatrical experience—was written here in Venice by St. Mark's *maestro di cappella*, Claudio Monteverdi (1567-1643).

▶ *In the north transept (left of the altar) is an area usually reserved for prayer. The worshippers are facing a big stone canopy, which houses a small painting of the Virgin Mary.*

Mosaics use gold backgrounds to reflect light in the dim church interior.

❽ Nicopeia (North Transept)

Venetians then and now pray to a painted wooden icon of Mary and Baby Jesus known as "Nicopeia," or Our Lady of Victory. Supposedly painted by the evangelist Luke, it was once enameled with bright paint and precious stones, and Mary was adorned with a crown and necklace of gold and jewels (now on display in the Treasury). For centuries, Nicopeia was venerated by the Byzantines, who asked Mary to protect them in battle. When Venetian Crusaders captured it, the icon came to protect Venice. This Madonna has helped the city persevere through plagues, wars, and crucial soccer games.

▶ *Inside the church are three sights, each requiring a separate admission. These let you experience the richness of Byzantium up close and learn about the mosaics. If interested, start with the tiny, two-room Treasury in the south transept.*

❾ Treasury (Tesoro)

The Treasury holds a beautiful collection of chalices, reliquaries, and jewels, most of them stolen from Constantinople. As Venice thought of itself as the granddaughter of Rome and the daughter of Byzantium, Venetians consider these treasures not stolen, but inherited. This is marvelous handiwork, but all the more marvelous for having been done when Western Europe was still mired in the Dark Ages.

The Legend (Mixed with a Little Truth) of Mark and Venice

Mark (died c. AD 68) was a Jewish-born Christian, and he might have actually met Jesus. He traveled with fellow convert Paul, eventually settling in Alexandria as the city's first Christian bishop. On a trip to Rome, Peter—Jesus' right-hand man—asked him to write down the events of Jesus' life. This became the Gospel of Mark.

During his travels, Mark stopped in the lagoon (in Aquileia on the north coast of the Adriatic), where he dreamed of a Latin-speaking angel who said, *"Pax tibi Marce, evangelista meus"* ("Peace to you, Mark, my evangelist"), promising him rest after death. Back in Alexandria, Mark was attacked by an anti-Christian mob. They tied him with ropes and dragged his body through the streets until he died.

Eight centuries later, his body lay in an Alexandrian church that was about to be vandalized by Muslim fanatics. Two Venetian traders on a business trip saved the relics from desecration by hiding them in a basket of pork—a meat considered unclean by Muslims—and quickly setting sail. The doge received the body, and in 832 they built the first church of St. Mark's to house it. After construction of the current church started in 1063, Mark's relics were temporarily lost, and it took another miracle to find them, hidden inside a column. Today, Venetians celebrate Mark on the traditional date of his martyrdom, April 25.

▶ *Upon entering, you'll be directed into the small room of the reliquaries in glass cases.*

Relics Room: The first display cases (to the left) contain a glass reliquary with the bones of Doge Orseolo (r. 976-978), who built the church that preceded the current structure, and the bones of St. George, the legendary dragon slayer.

Straight ahead, the glass case over the glowing alabaster altar contains elaborate gold-and-glass reliquaries holding relics of Jesus'

Passion—his torture and execution. The central reliquary showing Christ tied to a column and being whipped (from 1125) holds a stone from that very column he was tied to.

▶ *Now enter the…*

Main Room: Start with the large glass case in the center of the room. It holds the most precious Byzantine objects (mostly war booty brought here during the Fourth Crusade in 1204).

The first piece you encounter is a hanging lamp (with protruding seashells and fish) made from a fourth-century Roman rock crystal framed in 11th-century Byzantine metalwork. Just behind the lamp, a black bucket, carved in the fourth century with scenes of satyrs chasing nymphs, epitomizes the pagan world that was fading as Christianity triumphed.

Circling to the right, you'll come across a couple of rectangular golden icons with (extremely precious) blue lapis lazuli scenes of the Crucifixion. Next, browse the array of chalices made of amber-colored sardonyx, agate, and rock crystal, all trimmed in gold filigree.

Around back, see a display of a Byzantine specialty: enamel work (which we'll see at the Golden Altarpiece). The "Grotto of the Virgin" is made from a Roman-era piece of rock crystal sitting on a Byzantine-enamel pedestal, with a gilded Venetian Virgin.

And finally, find the jewel-encrusted icon of Archangel Michael—standing like an action hero, ready to conquer evil in the name of Christ.

▶ *Along the walls, find the following displays (working counterclockwise around the room).*

The first three glass cases have more bowls and urns from the three medieval cultures that cross-pollinated in the Eastern Mediterranean: Venetian, Byzantine, and Islamic.

Next, on a wooden pedestal, comes the Urn of Artaxerxes I (next to window in right wall). It once held the ashes of the great Persian king who ruled 2,500 years ago.

The next cases hold religious paraphernalia used for High Mass—chalices, reliquaries, candlesticks, and a 600-year-old ceremonial crosier (reminiscent of a shepherd's staff) still used today by the chief priest on holy days.

Next is the Ciborio di Anastasia (far left corner). The object may be a gift from "Anastasia," the name carved on it in Greek. She was a lady-in-waiting in the court of the emperor Justinian (483-565). Christian legend has it that she was so beautiful that Justinian (a married man) pursued her amorously, so she had to dress like a monk and flee to a desert monastery.

Moving to the next wall, you'll see two large golden panels that once fronted an altar. Flanking the panels are two golden candlesticks with amazing detail, from the smiling angels at the top all the way down to the roots. Nearby, see a photo of a Madonna adorned with the jewels, gold, and enamel that are used to grace the Nicopeia.

Finally, next to the Madonna, notice the granite column that extends below current floor level—you can see how the floor has risen as the basilica has settled in the last 1,000 years.

▶ *Return to the nave and follow the crowds through the turnstile and behind the main altar to the ...*

⑩ Golden Altarpiece (Pala d'Oro)

Under the green marble canopy, supported by four intricately carved, seventh-century alabaster columns (plundered from far away), sits the **high altar.** Inside the altar is an urn (not visible) with the mortal remains of Mark, the Gospel writer. (Look through the grate of the altar to read *Corpus Divi Marci Evangelistae*, or "Body of the Evangelist Mark.") He rests in peace, as an angel had promised him. Shh.

The **Golden Altarpiece** itself is a stunning golden wall made of 250 blue-backed enamels with religious scenes, all set in a gold frame and studded with 15 hefty rubies, 300 emeralds, 1,500 pearls, and assorted sapphires, amethysts, and topaz. The Byzantine-made enamels were part of the Venetians' plunder of 1204, subsequently pieced together by Byzantine craftsmen specifically for St. Mark's high altar. Get up close and find several details you might recognize:

In the center, Jesus as Ruler of the Cosmos sits on a golden throne, with a halo of jewels and pearls. Like a good Byzantine Pantocrator, he dutifully faces forward and gives his blessing while stealing a glance offstage at Mark ("Marcus") and the other saints.

Along the bottom row, Old Testament prophets show off the books of the Bible they've written. With halos, solemn faces, and elaborately creased robes, they epitomize the Byzantine icon style.

Mark's story is told in the vertical panels on each side. In the bottom left panel, Mark meets Peter (seated) at the gates of Rome. Peter gives Mark the eyewitness account of Jesus' life that Mark would write down in his Gospel. Mark's story ends in the bottom right panels with the two Venetian merchants returning by ship, carrying his coffin here in 829 to be laid to rest.

Cloisonné enameling like this was a Byzantine specialty. A piece of gold leaf is stamped with a design, then filled in with pools of enamel paste, and then fired. This kind of craftsmanship—and the social infrastructure that could afford it—made Byzantium seem like an enchanted world during Europe's dim Middle Ages.

After you've looked at some individual scenes, back up as far as this small room will allow and let yourself be dazzled by the whole picture—this "mosaic" of Byzantine greatness. This magnificent altarpiece sits on a swivel (notice the mechanism at its base) and is swung around on festival Sundays so the entire congregation can enjoy it, as Venetians have for so many centuries.

▶ *To reach the museum, return to the back of the church, near the main entrance, and climb the steep staircase. Follow signs to Museo e Loggia, or Loggia dei Cavalli, Museo. Buy your ticket at the top of the stairs.*

⓫ San Marco Museum (Museo di San Marco)

The museum's highlights are the original bronze horses, the view of the basilica interior, and the view of the square.

▶ *The museum loops you along on a suggested one-way route. Along the way, you'll see...*

Mosaic Fragments

These mosaics once hung in the church, but when they became damaged or aesthetically old-fashioned, they were replaced by more fashionable decor. You'll see mosaics from the church's earliest days (and most "Byzantine" style, c. 1070) to more recent times (1700s, more realistic and detailed). Many are accompanied by small photos that show where the fragment used to fit into a larger scene.

The mosaics—made from small tiles of stone or colored glass pressed into wet clay—were assembled on the ground, then cemented onto the walls. Artists drew the pattern on paper, laid it on the wet clay, and slowly cut the paper away as they replaced it with tiles.

Continuing on, down a set of stairs, you'll see other artwork and

The San Marco Museum offers this view down the church nave, with its Pentecost mosaic.

catch glimpses of the interior of the church from the north transept. Here you get a close-up view of the **Tree of Jesse mosaic,** showing Jesus' distant ancestor at the root and his mom at the top.

▶ *Continue on to the Sala dei Banchetti (WCs near the room's entrance).*

Sala dei Banchetti

This large, ornate room—once the doge's banquet hall—is filled with religious objects, tapestries, and carpets that once adorned the church; Burano-made lace vestments; illuminated music manuscripts; a doge's throne; and much more. In the center of the hall stands the most prestigious artwork here, the **Pala Feriale,** by Paolo Veneziano (1345). These 14 scenes painted on wood formed a cover for the basilica's Golden Altarpiece. The top row shows seven saints, including crucified Christ. Below are seven episodes in Mark's life, told with impressive realism.

▶ *Now the route doubles back, through displays of stone fragments from the church, finally arriving at the...*

Bronze Horses (La Quadriga)

Stepping lively in pairs and with smiles on their faces, these four bronze horses exude a spirited exuberance. They long stood in the most prominent spot in Venice—above the main door of St. Mark's Basilica, overlooking St. Mark's Square. Originally they were part of a larger ensemble shown pulling a chariot, *Ben-Hur* style.

The realism is remarkable: the halters around their necks, the bulging veins in their faces, their chest muscles, and the creases in their necks as they rear back. With flashing eyes, flaring nostrils, erect ears, and open mouths, they're the picture of equestrian energy.

These bronze statues are rare survivors of that remarkable ancient technology known as the lost-wax method. They were not hammered into shape by metalsmiths but cast—made by pouring molten bronze into clay molds. Each horse weighs nearly a ton. During the Dark Ages, barbarians melted most metal masterpieces down for reuse, but these survived. Originally gilded, they still have some streaks of gold leaf. Long gone are the ruby pupils that made their fiery eyes glisten in the sun.

The horses are old—much older even than Venice. Legend says they were made in Greece during the time of Alexander the

One of the treasures of the ancient world, this group has inspired Caesars, kings, and doges.

Great (fourth century BC). They were then taken by Nero to Rome. Constantine brought them to his new capital in Constantinople to adorn the chariot racecourse. In 1204, during the Fourth Crusade, the Venetians stole them. They placed them on the balcony of St. Mark's from where the doge would speak to his people—the horses providing a powerful backdrop. Six centuries later, Napoleon conquered Venice and took the horses. They stood atop a triumphal arch in Paris until Napoleon fell and they were returned to their "rightful" home in Venice.

In the 1970s, the horses made their shortest and final journey. With the threat of oxidation from polluted air, they were replaced by modern copies. The originals galloped for cover inside the basilica, where they are displayed today.

For all their travel, this fearsome foursome still seems fresh. They're more than just art. They stand as a testament to how each civilization conquers the previous one, assimilates the best elements from it, and builds upon it.

▶ *Belly up to the stone balustrade beyond the horses to survey the church interior.*

View of Church Interior

Scan the church, with its thousands of square yards of mosaics, then take a closer look at the Pentecost Mosaic (first dome above you). The unique design at the very top signifies the Trinity: throne (God), Gospels (Christ), and dove (Holy Spirit). The couples below the ring of apostles are the people of the world (I can find Judaea, Cappadocia, and Asia), who, despite their different languages, still understood the Spirit's message.

In medieval Venice, the balcony was for women, the nave for men, and the altar for the priests. Back then the rood screen (the fence with the 14 figures on it) separated the priest from the public. Looking down at the nave, appreciate the patterns of the mosaic floor—one of the finest in Italy—that unfurl like a Persian carpet.

Take a moment to view the models and drawings of the church at various stages of its history (near the balustrade).

▶ *The visit ends outside on the balcony overlooking St. Mark's Square.*

Loggia and View of St. Mark's Square

You'll be drawn repeatedly to the viewpoint of the square, but remember to look at the facade also to see how cleverly all the looted architectural elements blend together. Ramble among the statues of water-bearing slaves that serve as drain spouts. The horses are modern copies (note the 1978 date on the hoof of the horse to the right).

Be a doge, and stand aside the bronze horses overlooking St. Mark's Square. Under the gilded lion of St. Mark, and flanked by the four glorious horses, he inspired the Venetians to great things. Admire the mesmerizing, commanding view of this city, which so long ago was Europe's great superpower, and today is just a small town with a big history.

Doge's Palace Tour

Palazzo Ducale

Venice is a city of beautiful facades—palaces, churches, carnival masks—that cover darker interiors of intrigue and decay. The Doge's Palace, with its frilly pink exterior, hides the fact that the "Most Serene Republic" (as Venice called itself—"serene" meaning stable) was far from serene in its heyday.

The Doge's Palace housed the fascinating government of this rich and powerful empire. It also served as the home for the Venetian ruler known as the doge (pronounced "dohzh"), or duke. For four centuries (about 1150 to 1550), this was the most powerful half-acre in Europe. The doges wanted their palace to reflect the wealth and secular values of the Republic, impressing visitors and serving as a reminder that the Venetians were Number One in Europe.

ORIENTATION

Cost: €30 combo-ticket includes the Correr Museum, €1 fee for online reservation (timed-entry), covered by Museum Pass.

Hours: Daily 9:00-18:00, until 17:00 off-season, last entry one hour before closing.

Information: +39 041 271 5911, http://palazzoducale.visitmuve.it.

Avoiding Lines: There are three lanes for entering the Doge's Palace: for those with a ticket or a pass, for those without a ticket, and for those booked on a Secret Itineraries tour. To enter directly through the turnstile without a wait, buy your ticket online in advance or from the uncrowded Correr Museum across the square.

Getting There: The palace is next to St. Mark's Basilica, on the lagoon waterfront, and just off St. Mark's Square. Vaporetto stop: San Marco or San Zaccaria.

Tours: The **audioguide** is dry but informative (€5, 1.5 hours, need ID for deposit). The fine **Secret Itineraries Tour** lets you skip the line and covers rooms otherwise not open to the public (€28, 75 minutes; includes Doge's Palace admission but not Correr Museum, €15 with combo-ticket; reserve over the phone or online: +39 041 4273 0892, http://palazzoducale.visitmuve.it, €1 fee). Don't confuse this with the Doge's Hidden Treasures Tour, which isn't worth the cost.

Length of This Tour: Allow 1.5 hours.

Services: WCs are in the courtyard and halfway up the stairs to the balcony level. An elevator is available off the courtyard. Any bag bigger than a large purse must be checked (free) in the courtyard.

Eating: A café is off the palace courtyard. You'll find good sandwich bars and other cheap eats on and around Calle de le Rasse (two blocks behind the palace—see page 179).

Starring: Big rooms bare of furnishings but crammed with history, Tintoretto and Veronese masterpieces, and the doges.

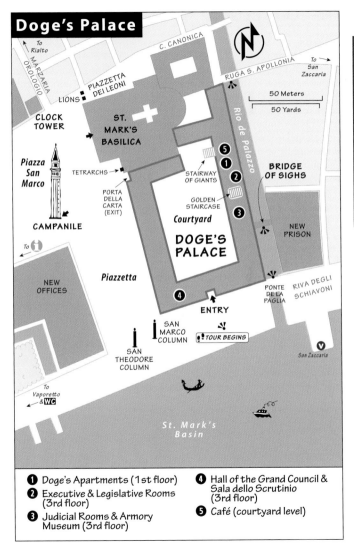

Doge's Palace

To Rialto

C. CANONICA

RUGA S. APOLLONIA

To San Zaccaria

MARZARIA OROLOGIO

PIAZZETTA DEI LEONI

LIONS

50 Meters

50 Yards

CLOCK TOWER

ST. MARK'S BASILICA

Rio de Palazzo

Piazza San Marco

TETRARCHS

PORTA DELLA CARTA (EXIT)

STAIRWAY OF GIANTS

❺

❶

❷

BRIDGE OF SIGHS

GOLDEN STAIRCASE

❸

CAMPANILE

Courtyard

DOGE'S PALACE

NEW PRISON

To

NEW OFFICES

Piazzetta

❹

PONTE DE LA PAGLIA

RIVA DEGLI SCHIAVONI

ENTRY

SAN MARCO COLUMN

TOUR BEGINS

SAN THEODORE COLUMN

San Zaccaria

To Vaporetto & WC

St. Mark's Basin

❶ Doge's Apartments (1st floor)
❷ Executive & Legislative Rooms (3rd floor)
❸ Judicial Rooms & Armory Museum (3rd floor)

❹ Hall of the Grand Council & Sala dello Scrutinio (3rd floor)
❺ Café (courtyard level)

THE TOUR BEGINS

Exterior

"The Wedding Cake," "The Tablecloth," or "The Pink House" is also sometimes known as the Doge's Palace. The style is called Venetian Gothic—a fusion of Italian Gothic with a delicate Islamic flair. The columns originally had bases on the bottoms, but these were covered over as the columns sank, and the square was built up over the centuries.

If you compare this lacy, top-heavy structure with the massive fortress-palaces of Florence, you realize the wisdom of building a city in the middle of the sea—you have no natural enemies except gravity. This unfortified palace in a city with no city wall was the doge's way of saying, "I am an elected and loved ruler. I do not fear my own people."

▶ *Enter the Doge's Palace from along the waterfront. After you pass through the turnstile, ignore the* Recommended Itinerary *signs for a moment, and enter the courtyard.*

Courtyard and Stairway of Giants (Scala dei Giganti)

Here in this vast space, you're surrounded by the buildings that housed Venice's ruling class. The courtyard is a hodgepodge of architectural styles, reflecting how the palace was refurbished repeatedly over the centuries: bare brick walls, round Renaissance arches, Baroque flourishes, and Gothic spires.

At one end of the courtyard, the palace is attached to the basilica, symbolically welding church and state. Both buildings have ugly brick behind a painted-lady veneer of marble. In this tour, we'll see the similarly harsh inner workings of an outwardly serene, polished republic.

Lacy, unfortified home of the doge | Grand entrance guarded by Neptune and Mars

▶ *Head to the far end of the courtyard (near the basilica) and stand at the foot of the grand staircase topped by two statues.*

Imagine yourself as a foreign dignitary on business to meet the doge. You'd enter the palace up these stairs topped with two nearly nude statues of, I think, Moses and Paul Newman (more likely Neptune and Mars, representing Venice's prowess at sea and at war). The doge and his aides would be waiting for you at the top, between the two statues and beneath the winged lion. No matter who you were—king, pope, or emperor—you'd have to hoof it up. The powerful doge would descend the stairs for no one.

Many doges were crowned right here, between the two statues. The doge was something like an elected king—which makes sense only in the dictatorial republic that was Venice. Technically, he was just a noble selected by other nobles to carry out their laws and decisions. Many doges tried to extend their powers and rule more as divine-right kings; others just put on their funny hats and accepted their role as figureheads and ceremonial ribbon-cutters.

▶ *Cross back to the entrance and follow the signs up the tourists' staircase to the first-floor balcony (loggia). Midway along the balcony, you'll find a face in the wall, the...*

Mouth of Truth

This fierce-looking androgyne opens his/her mouth, ready to swallow a piece of paper, hungry for gossip. Letterboxes like this (some with lions' heads) were scattered throughout the palace. Originally, anyone who had a complaint or suspicion about anyone else could accuse them anonymously (*denontie secrete*) by simply dropping a slip of paper in the mouth. This set the blades of justice turning inside the palace.

Mouth of Truth—the post box of doom

Golden Staircase with a 24-carat ceiling

Paintings by Titian, Veronese, and Tintoretto

Only the top Venetian painters decorated the Doge's Palace. It was once rich in Titians, but fires in the late 1500s destroyed nearly all the work by the greatest Venetian master. As the palace was hastily reconstructed, the empty spaces left by the Titians were quickly patched in with works by Veronese and Tintoretto.

Veronese used the best pigments available—made from minerals and precious stones—and his colors have survived vividly. These Veronese paintings are by the artist's hand and are fine examples of his genius. Tintoretto, on the other hand, didn't really have his heart in these commissions, and the pieces here were made by his workshop.

The paintings of the Doge's Palace are a study of long-ago Venice, with fine views of the old city and its inhabitants. The extravagant women's gowns in the paintings by Veronese show off a major local industry—textiles. While the paintings are not generally of masterpiece quality, they're historically interesting. They prove that in the old days, Venice had no pigeons.

▶ *A few steps toward Paul Newman is the entrance to the...*

Golden Staircase (Scala d'Oro)

The palace was architectural propaganda, designed to impress visitors. With its 24-karat gilded ceiling, it was something for them to write home about.

▶ *Start up the first few steps of the Golden Staircase. Midway up, at the first landing, turn right, which loops you through a dozen rooms (often closed). If they're open, enter and enjoy the...*

Doge's Apartments (Appartamento del Doge)

The dozen or so rooms on the first floor are where the doge actually lived. The blue-and-gold-hued Sala dei Scarlatti (Room 5) is typical of the palace's interior decoration: gold-coffered ceiling, big stone fireplace, silky walls with paintings, and a speckled floor. There's very little original furniture, as doges were expected to bring their own. Despite his high office, the doge had to obey several rules that bound him to the city. He couldn't leave the palace unescorted, he couldn't open official mail in private, and he and his family had to leave their own home and live in the Doge's Palace.

The large Room 6, the Sala dello Scudo (Shield Hall), is full of maps and globes. The main map illustrates the reach of Venice's maritime realm, which stretched across most of the eastern Mediterranean. With the maps in this room you can trace the eye-opening trip across Asia—from Italy to Greece to Palestine, Arabia, and "Irac"—of local boy Marco Polo (c. 1254-1325). This last map (at the far end of the room) is shown "upside-down," with south on top, giving you a glimpse of the Venetian worldview circa 1550. It depicts China, Taiwan (Formosa), and Japan (Giapan), while America is a nearby island made up of California and lots of Terre Incognite with *antropofagi* (cannibals).

In Room 7, the Sala Grimani, are several paintings of the lion of St. Mark, including the famous one by Vittore Carpaccio of a smiling lion (on the long wall). The lion holds open a book with these words, *"Pax Tibi Marce..."* ("Peace to you, Mark"), which, according to legend, were spoken by an angel welcoming St. Mark to Venice. In the background are the Doge's Palace and the Campanile.

▶ *The visitors route through the Doge's Apartments returns you to the Golden Staircase. Continue up the Golden Staircase to the third floor, which was the "public" part of the palace. The room right at the top of the stairs is the...*

Square Room (Atrio Quadrato)

The ceiling painting, **Justice Presenting the Sword and Scales to Doge Girolamo Priuli,** is by Jacopo Tintoretto. (Stand at the top of the painting for the full 3-D effect.) As you'll soon see, this palace is wallpapered with Titians, Tintorettos, and Veroneses. Many have the same theme: a doge, in his ermine cape, gold-brocaded robe, and funny one-horned hat with earflaps, kneeling in the presence of saints, gods, or mythological figures.

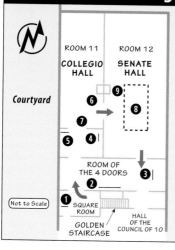

Executive & Legislative Rooms

ROOM 11
COLLEGIO HALL

ROOM 12
SENATE HALL

Courtyard

ROOM OF THE 4 DOORS

Not to Scale

SQUARE ROOM

GOLDEN STAIRCASE

HALL OF THE COUNCIL OF 10

❶ TINTORETTO – *Justice Presenting the Sword and Scales*

❷ TITIAN – *Doge Kneeling*

❸ TIEPOLO – *Venice Receiving Neptune*

❹ VERONESE – *The Rape of Europa*

❺ TINTORETTO – *Bacchus and Ariadne*

❻ VERONESE – *Discussion*

❼ VERONESE – *Mars and Neptune with Campanile and Lion*

❽ TINTORETTO – *Triumph of Venice*

❾ Clocks

▶ *Enter the next room.*

Room of the Four Doors (Sala delle Quattro Porte)

This was the central clearinghouse for all the goings-on in the palace. Visitors presented themselves here and were directed to their destination—the courts, councils, or the doge himself.

The room was designed by Andrea Palladio, the architect who did the impressive Church of San Giorgio Maggiore, across the Grand Canal from St. Mark's Square. On the intricate stucco ceiling, notice the feet of the women dangling down below the edge (above the windows), extending the illusion.

On the wall to the right of the door you entered from is a **painting by Titian** (ho-hum), showing a woman embodying Faith holding the Cross of Jesus, while a doge kneels with great piety. Notice old Venice in the misty distance under the cross. This is one of many paintings you'll see of doges in uncharacteristically humble poses—paid for, of course, by the doges themselves.

At the end of the room, find G. B. Tiepolo's well-known ***Venice Receiving Neptune*** high up on the wall above the windows. (This

G. B. Tiepolo's *Venice Receiving Neptune*—the city personified by a sensual woman

is a copy, but the original is often displayed on an easel nearby.) The painting shows Venice as a woman—Venice is always a woman to artists—reclining in luxury. She's dressed in the ermine cape and pearl necklace of a doge's wife (dogaressa). Crude Neptune, enthralled by the First Lady's beauty, arrives bearing a seashell bulging with gold ducats. A bored Venice points and says, "Put it over there with the other stuff."

▶ *Enter the small room with the big fireplace and several paintings.*

Ante-Collegio Hall (Sala dell'Anticollegio)

If the doge agreed to see you, you'd wait in this room—combing your hair, adjusting your robe, popping a breath mint, and preparing the gifts you'd brought. While you cooled your heels and warmed your hands at the elaborate fireplace, you might look at some of the paintings—among the finest in the palace and the world of art.

The Rape of Europa (on the wall opposite the fireplace), by Paolo Veronese, most likely shocked many small-town visitors with its risqué subject matter. Here Zeus, the king of the Greek gods, appears in the form of a bull with a foot fetish, seducing a beautiful bare-breasted earthling, while cupids spin playfully overhead.

Tintoretto's **Bacchus and Ariadne** (right of the fireplace) is another colorful display of Venice's sensual tastes. The God of Wine seeks a threesome, offering a ring to the mortal Ariadne, who's being crowned with stars by Venus, who turns slowly in zero gravity. The ring is the center of a spinning wheel of flesh, with three arms like spokes.

Veronese's *Rape of Europa* greeted palace visitors with a glimpse into the city's risqué tastes.

▶ *Enter the next room and approach your imaginary doge.*

Collegio Hall (Sala del Collegio)

Flanked by his cabinet of six advisers—one for each Venetian neighborhood—the doge would sit on the wood-paneled platform at the far end to receive ambassadors, who laid their gifts at his feet and pleaded their countries' cases. All official ceremonies, such as the ratification of treaties, were held here.

At other times, it was the "Oval Office" where the doge and his cabinet (the executive branch) would meet in private, pull files from the cabinets (along the right wall) regarding business with Byzantium, or rehearse a meeting with the pope. The wooden benches around the sides (where they sat) are original. The clock on the wall is a backward-running 24-hour clock with Roman numerals and a sword for its single hand.

The **ceiling** is gilded, with paintings by Veronese. These are not frescoes (painting on wet plaster), like those in the Sistine Chapel, but actual canvases painted in Veronese's studio and then placed on the ceiling.

The T-shaped painting of the woman admiring the spider web (on the ceiling, opposite the big window) represents the Venetian symbol of **Discussion.** You can imagine the webs of truth and lies woven in this room by the doge's scheming advisers.

In *Mars and Neptune with Campanile and Lion* (the ceiling painting near the entrance), Veronese presents four symbols of the Republic's strength—military, sea trade, city, and government (plus a cherub about to be circumcised by the Campanile).

▶ Enter the large Senate Hall.

Senate Hall (Sala del Senato)

This huge hall is where some 120 senators met to pass legislation. While the doge presided from the stage, senators mounted the podium (middle of the wall with windows) to address their colleagues.

Venice prided itself on its self-rule (independent of popes, kings, and tyrants), with most power placed in the hands of these annually elected noble men. Which branch of government really ruled? All of them. It was an elaborate system of checks and balances to make sure no one rocked the gondola, no one got too powerful, and the ship of state sailed smoothly ahead.

Tintoretto's large *Triumph of Venice* on the ceiling (central painting, best viewed from the top) is an allegory of the city in all her glory. Lady Venice is up in heaven with the Greek gods, while barbaric lesser nations swirl up to give her gifts and tribute. Do you get the feeling the Venetians were proud of their city?

Mars and Neptune with Campanile and Lion

Triumph of Venice oversees the Senate.

On the wall are two large **clocks,** one of which has the signs of the zodiac and phases of the moon. And there's one final oddity in this room, in case you hadn't noticed: In one of the wall paintings (above the entry door), there's actually a doge...not kneeling.

▶ *Exiting the Senate Hall, pass again through the Room of the Four Doors, then around the corner into a hall with a semicircular carved-wood platform.*

Hall of the Council of Ten (Sala del Consiglio dei Dieci)

The dreaded Council of Ten—10 judges, plus the doge and his six advisers—met here to dole out punishment to traitors, murderers, and "morals" violators.

Venice developed a worldwide reputation for swift, harsh, and secret justice. The Council of Ten had their own force of police officers, guards, spies, informers, and even assassins. It seemed no one was safe from the spying eye of the "Terrible Ten." You could be accused of crimes anonymously (by a letter dropped into a Mouth of Truth), swept off the streets, tried, judged, and thrown into the dark dungeons in the palace for the rest of your life without so much as a Miranda warning.

It was in this room that the Council decided who lived or died, and who was decapitated, tortured, or merely thrown in jail. The small, hard-to-find **door** leading off the platform (the fifth panel to the right of center) leads directly through secret passages to the prisons and torture chambers.

The large central ceiling painting by Veronese (a copy of the original stolen by Napoleon and still in the Louvre) shows **Jupiter Descending from Heaven to Strike Down the Vices,** redundantly informing the accused that justice in Venice was swift and harsh. Though the dreaded Council of Ten was eventually disbanded, today their descendants enforce the dress code at St. Mark's Basilica.

▶ *Pass through the next room, turn right, and head up the stairs to the Armory Museum.*

Armory Museum (L'Armeria)

The aesthetic of killing is beyond me, but I must admit I've never seen a better collection of halberds, falchions, ranseurs, targes, morions, and brigandines in my life. The weapons in these four rooms make

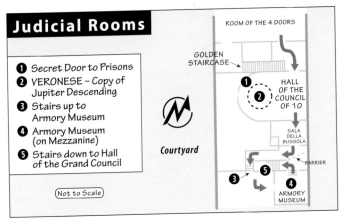

you realize the important role the military played in keeping the East-West trade lines open.

Room 1: In the glass case on the right, you'll see the suit of armor worn by the great Venetian mercenary general Gattamelata (far right, on horseback), as well as "baby's first armor" (how quickly they grow up!). A full suit of armor could weigh 66 pounds. Before gunpowder, crossbows (look up) were made still more lethal by turning a crank on the end to draw the bow with extra force.

Room 2: In the thick of battle, even horses needed helmets. The hefty broadswords were brandished two-handed by the strongest and bravest soldiers who waded into enemy lines. Opposite the window stands the fine armor of Henry IV, a 16th-century king of France. Behind him is a cell for VIP prisoners.

Room 3: On the walls and weapons, the "C-X" insignia means that this was the private stash of the "Council of Ten."

Room 4: In this room, rifles and pistols enter the picture. At the far (left) end of the room is a very, very early (17th-century) attempt at a 20-barrel machine gun. Don't miss the glass case in the corner, with a tiny crossbow, some torture devices (including an effective-looking thumbscrew), the wooden "devil's box" (a clever item that could fire in four directions at once), and a nasty, two-holed chastity belt. These disheartening "iron breeches" were worn by the devoted wife of the Lord of Padua.

▶ *Exit the Armory Museum. Go downstairs and turn left into the long hall with a wood-beam ceiling. You'll wind through some often-interesting exhibits before opening your eyes as wide as you can to see the...*

Hall of the Grand Council (Sala del Maggiore Consiglio)

It took a room this size to contain the grandeur of the Most Serene Republic. This huge room (175 by 80 feet) could accommodate up to 2,600 people at one time. The engineering is remarkable. The ceiling is like the deck of a ship—its hull is the rooftop, creating a huge attic above that.

The doge presided from the raised dais, while the nobles—the backbone of the empire—filled the center and lined the long walls. Nobles were generally wealthy men over 25, but the title had less to do with money than with long bloodlines. In theory, the doge, the Senate, and the Council of Ten were all subordinate to the Grand Council of nobles who met here to elect them.

On the wall over the doge's throne is Tintoretto's monsterpiece, **Paradise,** the largest painted canvas in Venice (570 square feet). Christ and Mary are at the top of heaven, surrounded by 500 people. It's rush hour in heaven, and all the good Venetians made it. Tintoretto worked on this in the last years of his long life. On the day it was finished, his daughter died. He got his brush out again and painted her as saint number 501. She's dead center with the blue skirt, hands clasped, getting sucked up to heaven.

Veronese's **Apotheosis of Venice** (on the ceiling at the Tintoretto end—view it from the top) is a typically unsubtle work showing Lady Venice being crowned a goddess by an angel.

Ringing the top of the hall are portraits, in chronological order,

Tintoretto's *Paradise*—500-plus figures

Siege of Constantinople

Hall of the Grand Council

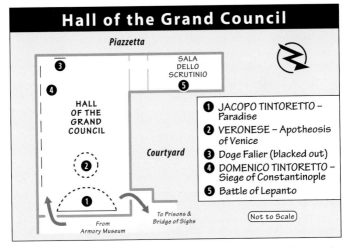

Piazzetta

SALA DELLO SCRUTINIO

HALL OF THE GRAND COUNCIL

Courtyard

1 JACOPO TINTORETTO – Paradise
2 VERONESE – Apotheosis of Venice
3 Doge Falier (blacked out)
4 DOMENICO TINTORETTO – Siege of Constantinople
5 Battle of Lepanto

To Prisons & Bridge of Sighs

From Armory Museum

Not to Scale

of the first 76 doges. The one at the far end that's blacked out is the notorious **Doge Marin Falier,** who opposed the will of the Grand Council in 1355. He was tried for treason, beheaded, and airbrushed from history.

Along the entire wall to the right of *Paradise,* a series of paintings called the *Siege of Constantinople* (by Tintoretto's son, Domenico) chronicles Venice's greatest military (if not moral) victory: the conquest of the fellow Christian city of Constantinople during the Fourth Crusade (1204, see sidebar on page 54). The sneaky Venetians attacked from the water's edge. Skillful Venetian oarsmen cozied their galleys right up to the dock, allowing soldiers to scoot along crossbeams attached to the masts and on to the top of the city walls. The gates are opened, the Byzantine emperor parades out to surrender, and tiny Doge Dandolo says, "Let's go in and steal some bronze horses."

Step into the adjoining **Sala dello Scrutinio.** The room's huge paintings burst with action. The enormous *Battle of Lepanto* depicts the great Venetian empire's last hurrah. The Venetians' sleek ships with skilled oarsmen plowed through the Ottoman navy to victory in 1571.

But Venice had already begun its long slide into historical oblivion. One by one, the Ottomans gobbled up Venice's trading outposts.

Finally, in 1797, the French general Napoleon marched into town shouting *"Liberté, égalité, fraternité,"* the Most Serene Republic was conquered, and the last doge was forced to abdicate.

▶ *Our final stop is the prisons. Consider reading about them here, where there are more benches and fewer rats.*

To reach the prisons, exit the Hall of the Grand Council by squeezing through the door to the left of Tintoretto's monsterpiece. Follow signs for Prigioni/Ponte dei Sospiri, *passing through several rooms. You'll reach a narrow staircase going down, following signs to the prisons. (It's near Room 31; if you miss it, you'll end up at the bookshop near the exit.) Cross the covered Bridge of Sighs over the canal to the prisons.*

Prisons

Musty, humid, and clammy, with heavy stone walls and thick iron bars—these are rooms that wouldn't rate a single star in a Rick Steves book. These were the palace's special dungeons. In the privacy of his own home, a doge could oversee the sentencing, torturing, and jailing of political opponents.

Circle the cells. Justice here was harsh. The cells consisted of cold stone with heavily barred windows, a wooden plank for a bed, a shelf, and a bucket. You can feel the cold and damp.

In the far corner of the complex, look closely at the windowsills of the cells. There are carvings scratched by prisoners, dating from olden days up until the 1920s.

Explore the rest of the prisons. You can descend lower to the notorious cells called "the wells" because they were so deep, wet, and cramped. Or stay on this floor, where there's a room of displays, including ceramic shards found in archaeological digs. Adjoining that are more cells, including one (the farthest) where you can see the bored prisoners' compelling and sometimes artistic sketches. The singing gondoliers outside are a reminder of how tantalizingly close these pitiful prisoners were to one of the world's finest cities.

▶ *Wherever you roam, you'll end up where you entered. Head back over the bridge that once carried prisoners to their grim fate, and stand in the middle.*

It's a romantic scene today, but the "sighs" from this bridge once came from condemned prisoners.

Bridge of Sighs

Gaze through the stonework windows at the view of Venice. According to romantic legend, criminals were tried and sentenced in the palace, then marched across the canal to the dark prisons. On this bridge, they got one last look at Venice. They gazed out at the sky, the water, and the beautiful buildings, and...sighed.

▶ *Take one last look at all the tourists and the heavenly Church of San Giorgio Maggiore, heave one last sigh, and leave the palace.*

Frari Church Tour

Basilica di Santa Maria Gloriosa dei Frari

For me, this church offers the best art-appreciation experience in Venice, because so much of its great art is in situ—right where it was designed to be seen, rather than hanging in museums.

The church was built by the Franciscan order and consecrated in 1492. Franciscan men and women were inspired by St. Francis of Assisi (c. 1182-1226), who dedicated himself to a nonmaterialistic life-style. The spirit of St. Francis of Assisi warms both the church of his "brothers" (*frari*) and the art that decorates it. The Franciscan love of all of creation—Nature and Humanity—later inspired Renaissance painters to capture the beauty of the physical world and human emotions, showing worshippers the glory of God in human terms.

ORIENTATION

Cost: €5.

Hours: Mon-Thu 9:00-19:30, Fri until 23:00, Sat until 18:00, Sun 13:00-18:00, shorter hours in winter.

Information: +39 041 272 8611, http://www.basilicadeifrari.it.

Dress Code: Modest dress is recommended.

Getting There: It's near the San Tomà vaporetto and *traghetto* stops. From the dock, follow signs to *Scuola Grande di San Rocco*. For a pleasant stroll from the Rialto Bridge, take the 📖 Rialto to Frari Church Walk.

Tours: You can rent an **audioguide** for €2 or 🎧 download my free Frari Church **audio tour.**

Length of This Tour: Allow one hour.

Eating: The church square is ringed with small, simple, reasonably priced cafés. The Bottega del Caffè Dersut (around to the left, facing the side of the church, inside seating only) serves salads and fresh sandwiches.

Nearby: For efficient sightseeing, combine your visit with the nearby Scuola San Rocco and the Ca' Rezzonico, a seven-minute walk away.

Starring: Titian, Giovanni Bellini, Paolo Veneziano, and Donatello.

THE TOUR BEGINS

▶ *Enter the church, let your eyes adjust, and stand just inside the door with a good view down the long nave toward the altar.*

❶ Church Interior and Choir, 1250-1443

The simple, spacious (110-yard-long), well-lit Gothic church—with rough wood crossbeams and a red-and-white color scheme—is truly a remarkable sight in a city otherwise crammed with exotic froufrou. Traditionally, churches in Venice were cross-shaped, but because the Franciscans were an international order, they weren't limited to Venetian tastes. This new T-shaped footprint featured a long, lofty nave—flooded with light and suited to large gatherings—where common people heard sermons. The T, or tau, is the symbol of the

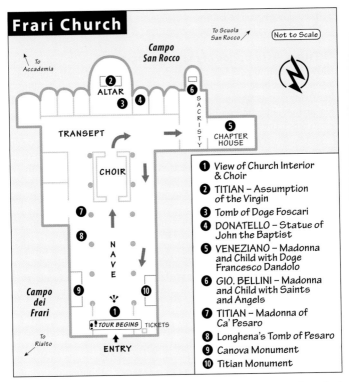

Frari Church

Not to Scale

To Scuola San Rocco

To Accademia

Campo San Rocco

ALTAR ❷

❸ ❹

❻ SACRISTI

TRANSEPT

❺ CHAPTER HOUSE

CHOIR

❼

❽

NAVE

Campo dei Frari

❾

❿

To Rialto

❶ TOUR BEGINS TICKETS

ENTRY

❶ View of Church Interior & Choir

❷ TITIAN – Assumption of the Virgin

❸ Tomb of Doge Foscari

❹ DONATELLO – Statue of John the Baptist

❺ VENEZIANO – Madonna and Child with Doge Francesco Dandolo

❻ GIO. BELLINI – Madonna and Child with Saints and Angels

❼ TITIAN – Madonna of Ca' Pesaro

❽ Longhena's Tomb of Pesaro

❾ Canova Monument

❿ Titian Monument

Franciscan order. St. Francis chose the tau as his personal symbol, wearing it on his clothes and using it in place of his signature.

The carved-marble choir area in the center of the nave allowed friars to hold smaller, more intimate services. As worshippers entered the church and looked down the long nave to the altar, they were greeted by Titian's glorious painted altarpiece—then, as now, framed by the arch of the choir entrance. When Titian was chosen to paint the altarpiece, he surely had this perspective in mind.

▶ *Walk prayerfully toward Titian's heavenly Virgin, passing through the gorgeously carved wooden stalls of the 1480s* **choir.** *Notice the* *fine inlay above the chairs, showing the Renaissance enthusiasm for Florentine-style depth and perspective.*

❷ Titian, *Assumption of the Virgin*, 1516-1518

Glowing red and gold like a stained-glass window, this altarpiece sets a tone of exuberant beauty. At the end of her life (though looking 17 here), Mary was miraculously "assumed" into heaven. As cherubs lift her up to meet a Jupiter-like God, the stunned apostles on Earth reach up to touch the floating bubble of light.

The church is littered with chapels and tombs "made possible by the generous financial support" of rich people who donated to the Franciscans for the good of their souls (and usually for tomb-topping statues of themselves, as well). But the Franciscans didn't sell their main altar; instead they hired the new whiz artist, Titian, to create a dramatic altar painting.

Unveiled in 1518, the work scandalized a Venice accustomed to simpler, more contemplative church art. The rich colors, twisting poses, and mix of saccharine angels with blue-collar apostles were unheard of. Most striking, this Virgin is fully human—a real woman in the golden glow of heaven, not a stiff icon on a throne. The Franciscans thought this woman aroused excitement rather than spirituality. They agreed to pay Titian only after the Holy Roman Emperor offered to buy the altar if they refused.

In a burst of youthful innovation, Titian (c. 1490-1576) had rewritten the formula for church art, hinting at changes to come with the Mannerist and Baroque styles. He energized the scene with a complex composition, overlapping a circle (Mary's bubble) and a triangle (draw a line from the apostle reaching up to Mary's face and down the other side) on three horizontal levels (God in heaven, Man on Earth, Mary in between). Together these elements draw our eyes from the swirl of arms and legs to the painting's focus—the radiant face of a triumphant Mary, "assumed body and soul into heaven."

▶ *Flanking the painting are marble tombs lining the walls. On the wall to the right of the altar is the...*

❸ Tomb of Doge Foscari, 15th Century

This heavy, ornate tomb honors the great Venetian who ruled Venice at the peak of its power. Doge Francesco Foscari (1373-1457) assumed

Titian's *Assumption*—as she rises to heaven, Mary radiates spirituality through physical beauty

control of the city's powerful seafaring empire and then tried to expand it onto the mainland. Unfortunately, he ended up battling Milan in a 31-year war of attrition that swept through northern Italy. Meanwhile, on the unprotected eastern front, the Ottomans took Constantinople (1453) and scuttled Venice's trade. Venice's long slide into historical oblivion had begun. Financially drained city fathers forced Foscari to resign, turn in his funny hat, and hand over the keys to the Doge's Palace.

▶ *In the first chapel to the right of the altar, you'll find...*

❹ Donatello, Statue of John the Baptist, 1438

In the center of the altarpiece, the cockeyed prophet of the desert—emaciated from his breakfast of bugs 'n' honey and dressed in animal skins—freezes mid-rant when he spies something in the distance. His jaw goes slack, he twists his face and raises his hand to announce the coming of...the Renaissance.

Florentine expatriates in Venice commissioned the Florentine Donatello to make this wooden statue in a style reminiscent of home. The Renaissance began in Florence, where Donatello (1386-1466) created realistic statues with a full range of human emotions. This warts-and-all John the Baptist is harshly realistic, with muted colors. By contrast, Venetian art was painterly, with a soft focus, and beautiful, with bright colors.

▶ *Enter the sacristy through the door at the far end of the right transept. You'll bump into an elaborate altar crammed with **reliquaries,** including a vial supposedly containing a drop of Christ's blood. Facing the relic, enter the room to the right.*

Donatello's bold *John the Baptist* (center)

Bellini's *Madonna* in an illusory niche

Veneziano's *Madonna*—solemn, icon-like faces and neutral background show Byzantine roots.

❺ Paolo Veneziano, *Madonna and Child with Doge Francesco Dandolo*, c. 1339

Paolo Veneziano (literally, "Paul the Venetian") was the first "name" artist in Venice, the man who helped shape the distinctive painting style of his city. Veneziano paints Byzantine icons and sets them in motion. Baby Jesus turns to greet a kneeling Doge Dandolo, while rosy-cheeked Mary turns to acknowledge the doge's wife. None other than St. Francis presents "Francis" (Francesco) Dandolo to the Madonna. Both he and St. Elizabeth (on the right) bend at the waist and gesture as naturally as 14th-century icons can.

▶ *This room also has a **clock** intricately carved from a single piece of wood. Now return to the relics room and the glowing altarpiece at the end of the room.*

❻ Giovanni Bellini, *Madonna and Child with Saints and Angels*, 1488

This sacristy and Bellini masterpiece were funded by the Pesaro family, who negotiated an acceptable price for their family tomb.

Mary sits on a throne under a half-dome, propping up Baby Jesus, flanked by saints and serenaded by musician angels. Bellini (c. 1430-1516), the father of the Venetian Renaissance, had learned the budding realism of Veneziano, but he took it to another level. He painted fake columns and a dome to match the real ones in the gold frame, making the painting seem to be an extension of the room. He completes the illusion with glimpses of open sky in the background. Next, he fills the artificial niches with symmetrically posed, thoughtful saints—left to right, find Saints Nicholas, Peter, Mark, and Sean Connery (Benedict).

Bellini combined the meditative poses of the Venetian Byzantine tradition with Renaissance improvements in modern art. He helped pioneer the transition from painting with medieval tempera (egg yolk-based) to painting in oil (pigments dissolved in vegetable oil). Oils allowed a subtler treatment of colors because artists could apply them in successive layers. And because darker colors aren't so muddy when painted in oil, they "pop"—effectively giving the artist a brighter palette.

Bellini virtually invented the formula (later to be broken by his precocious pupil, Titian) for Venetian altarpieces. Instead of just standing around, his saints seem to interact in a holy conversation (*Sacra Conversazione*).

Renaissance humanism demanded Madonnas and saints that were accessible and human. Bellini delivers, but places them in a physical setting so beautiful that it creates its own mood of serene holiness. The scene is lit from the left, but nothing casts a harsh shadow—Mary and the babe are enveloped in a glowing aura of reflected light from the golden dome. The beauty is in the details—the writing in the dome, the red brocade backdrop, the swirls in the marble steps, and the angels' dimpled legs.

Musician angels serenade Baby Jesus from below.

▶ *Return to the nave and head left, toward the door you entered through.*
Just past the choir, look right and find Titian's colorful painting.

❼ Titian, *Madonna of Ca' Pesaro*, 1519-1526

Titian's second altarpiece for the Frari Church displays all that he'd
learned from his forebears. Like his teacher, Bellini, he puts Mary
(seated) and baby (standing) on a throne, surrounded by saints having
a holy conversation. Also like Bellini, he paints fake columns that echo
the church's real ones.

But wait. Mary is off-center, Titian's idealized saints mingle with
Venetians sporting five o'clock shadows, and the stairs run diagonally away from us. Mary sits not on a throne but on a pedestal. Baby
Jesus is restless. The precious keys of St. Peter seem to dangle unno-
ticed. These things upset traditional Renaissance symmetry, but they
turn a group of figures into a true scene. St. Peter (center, in blue and
gold, with book) looks down at Jacopo Pesaro, who kneels to thank
the Virgin for his recent naval victory over the Ottomans (1502). A
flag-carrying lieutenant drags in a turbaned captive. Meanwhile, St.
Francis talks to Baby Jesus while gesturing down to more members of
the Pesaro family. The little guy looking out at us (lower right) is the
Pesaro descendant who administered the trust fund to keep prayers
coming for his dead uncle.

Titian combines opposites: a soft-focus Madonna with photorealistic portraits, chubby winged angels with a Muslim prisoner, and
a Christian cross with a battle flag. In keeping with the spirit of St.
Francis' humanism, Titian lets mere mortals mingle with saints. And
we're right there with them.

▶ *Let's see some monuments, starting with one made for another Pesaro*
ancestor. It's the hard-to-miss tomb with black statues wearing ragged
white clothes.

❽ Longhena's Tomb of Pesaro

This eye-catching wall of stone was built for the next generation of
wealthy Pesaro family members, and honors the only one to become
a doge. It's the work of Baldassare Longhena, the same man who designed the over-the-top La Salute church. As the Renaissance world
moved into the Baroque, the style became more busy, exuberant,
and awe-inspiring. Longhena's (politically incorrect) black statues

Madonna of Ca' Pesaro—saints mingle with Venetians, making the heavenly seem real

Canova Monument—its greatest sculptor

Titian Monument—Venice's greatest painter

represent African prisoners who seem to support the upper story on their brawny shoulders (cushioned by pillows), where Doge Pesaro oversees it all.

▶ *Contrast Longhena's emotional Baroque tomb from the 1600s with the calmer Neoclassical lines of the 1700s in the next tomb over, the pyramid-shaped...*

❾ Canova Monument, 1827

Antonio Canova (1757-1822, see his portrait above the door) was Venice's greatest sculptor. He created gleaming white, highly polished statues of beautiful Greek gods and goddesses in the Neoclassical style. (See several of his works at the Correr Museum.)

The pyramid shape is timeless, suggesting pharaohs' tombs and the Christian Trinity. Mourners, bent over with grief, shuffle up to pay homage to the master artist. Even the winged lion is choked up.

Canova himself designed this pyramid-shaped tomb, not for his own use but as the tomb of an artist he greatly admired: Titian. But the Frari picked another design for Titian's tomb, so Canova used the pyramid for an Austrian princess...in Vienna. After his death, Canova's pupils copied the design here to honor their master. In fact, Canova isn't buried here. But inside the tomb's open door, you can (barely) see an urn, which contains his heart.

▶ *We'll finish with a monument directly across the nave from the Canova Monument—commemorating Venice's greatest artist.*

❿ Titian Monument, 1852

The enormous carved marble monument celebrates both the man (the center statue shows Titian with a beard and crown of laurels) and his famous paintings (depicted in the background reliefs).

Titian was the greatest Venetian painter, excelling equally in inspirational altarpieces, realistic portraits, joyous mythological scenes, and erotic female nudes.

He moved to Venice as a child, studying first as a mosaic-maker and then under Giovanni Bellini and Giorgione before establishing his own bold style, which featured teenage Madonnas (see a relief of *The Assumption of the Virgin* behind Titian). He became wealthy and famous, traveling Europe to paint stately portraits of kings and nobles, and colorful, sexy works for their bedrooms. Titian resisted the temptation of big money that drew so many of his contemporary Venetian artists to Rome. Instead he always returned to his beloved Venice (see winged lion on top)...and favorite Frari Church.

In his old age, Titian painted dark, tragic masterpieces, including the *Pietà* (see relief in upper left) that was intended for his tomb but ended up in the Accademia. Nearing 90, he labored to finish the *Pietà* as the plague enveloped Venice. Over a quarter of the population died, including Titian's son. Heartbroken, Titian died soon afterward, in August 1576. He was buried in the Frari, his grave barely marked. Three centuries later, this grandiose monument was built to remember and honor this great Venetian.

▶ *Before returning to the mobs, why not explore some back lanes and lonely canals from here and enjoy a softer, more meditative side of town?*

St. Mark's to Rialto Loop Walk

Just a few right and left turns (simple!) can get you from St. Mark's Square to the Rialto Bridge via a completely different route from the one most tourists take. Along the way, take in some lesser sights and appreciate the reality of Venice today.

Venice's population is half what it was just 30 years ago. Sad, yes, but imagine raising a family here: Apartments are small, high up, and expensive. Home-improvement projects require miles of red tape. Running a simple errand can mean crossing arched bridges while pushing a child in a stroller and carrying a day's worth of groceries.

On the other hand, those who stay couldn't imagine living anywhere else. This walk may help you understand why.

ORIENTATION

Length of This Walk: Allow one hour for a leisurely walk.

San Moisè Church: Free, Mon-Sat 9:30-12:30 & 15:30-19:30, Sun 15:30-19:30.

La Fenice Opera House: €11 for dry 45-minute audioguide tour, generally open daily 9:30-18:00, theater box office open daily 10:00-17:00.

Rialto Market: The souvenir stalls are open daily, the produce market is closed on Sunday, and the fish market is closed on Sunday and Monday. The market is lively only in the morning.

THE WALK BEGINS

St. Mark's Square

▶ *From the square, walk to the waterfront and stop between the two columns. You're walking on recently raised Venice—in 2006, the stones were taken up and six inches of extra sand put down to minimize flooding.*

You're at the front porch of Venice. Survey this grand scene with your back to the water. It reflects the Renaissance ideal of an urban layout: A proper city needs a formal entry. These pillars say "welcome to an aristocratic republic." The library (on your left) represents wisdom. The palace (right), with Lady Justice (never blindfolded in Venice) on top, represents righteousness. Medieval towns were cluttered. A grand Renaissance city has grand vistas. At the far end, the Clock Tower lets all know how much daylight is left ("XXIIII" is not set at midnight but changes with sunset). This monumentality wasn't always here. Before the 16th century there was no library. That's where you'd find the baker, butcher, and cheese shops.

▶ *Now, turn left to walk past the library, heading for a white pavilion.*

Beyond the library stands the old mint—looking pretty Fort Knox-y. In the 16th century the Venetian ducat—the dollar of Europe—was minted here.

Along the busy waterfront, you'll see the various boats that ply Venice's waters. Classic wooden motorboats operating as water taxis. Gondolas ferrying lovestruck tourists. Hotel shuttle boats bringing guests here from distant, $700-a-night hotels.

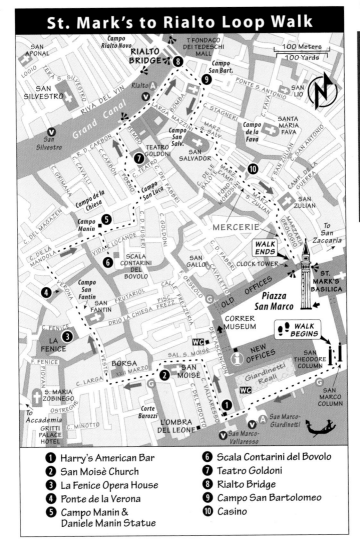

St. Mark's to Rialto Loop Walk

1. Harry's American Bar
2. San Moisè Church
3. La Fenice Opera House
4. Ponte de la Verona
5. Campo Manin & Daniele Manin Statue
6. Scala Contarini del Bovolo
7. Teatro Goldoni
8. Rialto Bridge
9. Campo San Bartolomeo
10. Casino

Run the gauntlet of souvenir stands to the entrance to the **Giardinetti Reali** (Royal Gardens, once the site of a huge grain-storage depot that was destroyed by Napoleon). The grounds (with ample benches) offer some precious greenery in a city built of stone on mud.

After the park entrance, the walkway takes you to a cute 18th-century former coffeehouse pavilion. Go around the left side of the pavilion and—from atop the bridge—look across the mouth of the Grand Canal to view the big dome of La Salute Church. The guy balancing a bronze ball on one foot is on top of the old Customs House, which now houses the Punta della Dogana contemporary art museum.

▶ *Twelve steps down and 20 yards ahead on the right is…*

❶ Harry's American Bar

Hemingway put this bar on the map by making it his hangout in the late 1940s. Today, you'll see plenty of dressed-up Americans looking around for celebrities. The discreet (and overpriced) restaurant upstairs is where the glitterati hang out. The street-level bar is for gawkers. If you wear something a bit fancy (or artsy bohemian), you can pull up a stool at the tiny bar by the entrance and pay too much for a Bellini (prosecco and peach puree), which was invented right here.

▶ *Head inland down Calle Vallaresso, one of Venice's most exclusive streets, past fancy boutiques such as Tiffany, Brunello Cucinelli, and Roberto Cavalli. At the T intersection, turn left and head west on Salizada San Moisè (which becomes Calle Larga XXII Marzo)—the Fifth Avenue of Venice with Gucci, Prada, Versace, and company. (A left turn down Calle del Ridotto leads to the fine, recommended canalfront bar, L'Ombra del Leone.) Continue to the first bridge and a square dominated by the fancy facade of a church. Climb the bridge and,*

The waterfront by St. Mark's Square

Harry's Bar—overpriced "celebrity" haunt

San Moisè Church

"The Phoenix," a classic opera house

against a soundtrack of tourists negotiating with hustling gondoliers, look back at the ornate...

❷ San Moisè Church

This is the parish church for St Mark's; because of tourist crowds at the basilica, this is where the community worships. While it's one of Venice's oldest churches, dating from the 10th century (note the old tower on the right), its busy facade is 17th-century Baroque. This was an age when big shots who funded such projects expected to see their faces featured (see the bust of Mr. Fini in the center—flanked by tombs of his brother and nephew all actually buried into the facade). Moses (Moisè) caps the facade.

Inside, the altarpiece depicts Mount Sinai, with Moses (kneeling) receiving the two tablets with the Ten Commandments. The alcove to the left of the altar has Tintoretto's 16th-century *Christ Washing the Disciples' Feet*.

▶ *Continue over the bridge, down Calle Larga XXII Marzo, a big street that seems too wide and large for Venice. It was created during the 19th century by filling in a canal. You can make out the outline of the sidewalks that once flanked the now-gone canal. Pass by the Vivaldi look-alikes selling concert tickets and vendors illegally selling knock-offs of Prada bags.*

Halfway down the street, after passing the grand Borsa (the former stock exchange), turn right on tiny Calle del Sartor da Veste. Go straight, crossing a bridge. At the next square, you'll find...

❸ La Fenice Opera House (Gran Teatro alla Fenice)

Venice's famed opera house, completed in 1792 (read the "MDCCXCII" on the facade), was started as a business venture by a group of nobles who recognized that Venice was short on entertainment opportunities for the well-heeled set.

La Fenice was reduced to a hollowed-out shell by a disastrous fire in 1996. After a vigorous restoration campaign, "The Phoenix"—true to its name—has risen again from the ashes. La Fenice resumed opera productions in 2004, opening with *La Traviata*. The theater is usually open daily to the public.

Venice is one of the cradles of the art form known as opera. An opera is a sung play and a multimedia event, blending music, words, story, costume, and set design. Some of the great operas were first performed here in this luxurious setting. Verdi's *Rigoletto* (1851) and *La Traviata* (1853) were actually commissioned by La Fenice. The man who put words to some of Mozart's opera tunes was a Venetian, Lorenzo da Ponte, who drew inspiration from the city's libertine ways and joie de vivre. In recent years, La Fenice's musical standing was overshadowed by its reputation as a place for the wealthy to parade in furs and jewels.

▶ *Passing La Fenice, continue north along the same street (now called Calle de la Verona), to a small bridge over a quiet canal.*

❹ Ponte de la Verona

Pause atop this bridge, where reflections can make you wonder which end is up. Looking above you, see bridges of stone propping up leaning buildings.

People actually live in Venice. Notice their rooftop gardens, their laundry, their plumbing, the electricity lines snaking into their apartments, and the rusted iron bars and bolts that hold their crumbling homes together. On one building, find centuries-old relief carvings—a bearded face and a panel of an eagle with its prey. Below you is an old water gate indicating that this was once a merchant's house.

While many Venetians own (and love) their own boats, parking watercraft is a huge problem. Getting a spot is tough, and when you finally find one, it's very expensive and rarely near your apartment.

People once swam freely in the canals. Find the sign that reads *Divieto di Nuoto* ("swimming not allowed").

View from Ponte de la Verona—a slice of everyday life that's both charming and crumbling

▶ *Continue north. At the T intersection, turn right on Calle de la Man-dola. You'll cross over a bridge into a spacious square dominated by a statue and an out-of-place modern building.*

❺ Campo Manin

The centerpiece of the square is a **statue of Daniele Manin** (1804-1857), one of a group of patriotic visionaries who foresaw the unifi-cation of Italy (the Risorgimento) 20 years before it happened. The statue faces the red house Manin lived in.

▶ *Our next stop, the Scala Contarini del Bovolo, is a block south of here, with yellow signs pointing the way. Facing the Manin statue, turn right and exit the square down an alley. Turn left with the street, then immediately follow yellow signs to the right, into a courtyard with one of Venice's hidden treasures.*

❻ Scala Contarini del Bovolo

Spiraling up the facade of an old palazzo, the *scala* (staircase) is a cylindrical brick tower with five floors faced with white limestone banisters.

Built in 1499, the external staircase broadcast the wealth of the palazzo owners and saved interior space for rooms. Architecture buffs admire the successful blend of a Gothic building with a Renaissance staircase. The garden is a graveyard of old cistern wellheads.

If the tower is open, you can pay €8 to wind your way up the "snail shell" (*bovolo* in the local dialect). It's 113 steps to the top, where you're rewarded with views of the Venetian skyline.

▶ *Unwind and return to the Manin statue. Continue east, circling around the right side of the big Cassa di Risparmio bank, marveling*

Daniele Manin, 19th-century patriot

The photogenic Scala Contarini del Bovolo

The Rialto Bridge, lined with shops, is the geographic "heart" of fish-shaped Venice.

at its Modernist ugliness. At Campo San Luca, walk halfway through the square, then turn left (north) on Calle del Forno. Heading north, glance 20 yards down the street to the right at the flag-bedecked...

❼ Teatro Goldoni

Though this theater dates from the 1930s, there's been a theater here since the 1500s, when Venice was at the forefront of secular entertainment. Many of Carlo Goldoni's (1707-1793) groundbreaking comedies were first performed here. Today, Teatro Goldoni is still a working theater of mainly Italian productions.

▶ *Continue north on Calle del Forno. You're very close to the Grand Canal. Keep going north. At the small square, jog left and then right onto a lane that leads past a big modern Co-op supermarket to the Grand Canal. Walk right out to the end of the small wooden pier for a grand view. On your right is the...*

❽ Rialto Bridge

Of Venice's more than 400 bridges, only four cross the Grand Canal. Rialto was the first among these four.

The original Rialto Bridge, dating from 1180, was a platform supported by boats tied together. It linked the political side (Palazzo Ducale) of Venice with the economic center (Rialto). Rialto, which takes its name from *rivo alto* (high bank), was one of the earliest Venetian settlements. When Venice was Europe's economic super-power, this was where bankers, brokers, and merchants conducted their daily business.

Rialto Bridge II was a 13th-century wooden drawbridge. It was replaced in 1588 by the current structure, with its bold single arch (spanning 160 feet) and arcades on top designed to strengthen the stone span. Its immense foundations stretch 650 feet on either side. Heavy buildings were then built atop the foundations to hold every-thing in place. The Rialto remained the only bridge crossing the Grand Canal until 1854.

Marking the geographical center of Venice (midway down the Grand Canal), the Rialto is the most sensible location for retail shops. The government built it with the (accurate) expectation that it'd soon pay for itself with rent from the shops built into it. Like the (older) Ponte Vecchio in Florence, the Rialto was originally lined with luxury gold and jewelry shops. The bridge is cleverly designed to generate maximum rent: three lanes, two rows of 12 shops each, with a ware-house area above each shop under the lead-and-timber roof.

Reliefs of the Venetian Republic's main mascots, St. Mark and St. Theodore, crown the arch. Barges and vaporetti run the busy water-ways below, and merchants vie for tourists' attention on top.

The Rialto has long been a symbol of Venice. Aristocratic inhabit-ants built magnificent palaces just to be near it. The poetic Lord Byron swam to it all the way from Lido Island. And thousands of marriage proposals have been sealed right here, with a kiss, as the moon floated over La Serenissima.

▶ *From here, you can continue this walk and return to St. Mark's Square or pick up my Rialto to Frari Church Walk (next chapter). From the base of the Rialto Bridge (on the San Marco side), go 100 yards directly to...*

⑨ Campo San Bartolomeo

This square is one of the city's main crossroads. Locals routinely meet at the **statue of Carlo Goldoni,** the beloved and innovative 18th-century playwright. The pharmacy on this square (marked by a green cross) keeps an electronic counter in its window, ticking down the population of Venice as it shrinks.

▶ *Head to the right 100 yards, down Via 2 Aprile, setting your sights on the green and red umbrellas on the corner. They mark a stretch of town once famous for selling umbrellas and handbags. From there, turn left and follow the crowds 100 yards more along Marzaria San Salvador, a.k.a. the...*

Mercerie

You're in the city's high-rent district. The Mercerie (or "Marzarie," in Venetian dialect) is a string of connecting streets lined mostly with tacky tourist shops. Much of the glass displayed here is Chinese, not Venetian. (If you're shopping for glass that's actually made in Venice, look for the Murano seal.)

▶ *When you get to the yellow two-way arrow "directing" you to San Marco, head right and then follow the flow left another 100 yards until you reach a bridge that makes for a fun gondola-viewing perch. At the top of the bridge, belly up to the railing on the left. Above the arcade on your left is the little iron balcony of the city's best-preserved...*

⑩ Casino

While humble from the outside, the interior is a great example of a classic Venetian space. If the windows are open, spy the lacy pastel and stucco ceilings inside. Though only a few of Venice's casinos still exist, the city once had over a hundred of these "little houses"—city-center retreats for the palazzo-dwelling set. For many patricians, they served as 18th-century man caves, used for entertaining, gambling, and/or intimate encounters. For well-to-do women, casinos provided

Playwright Carlo Goldoni

Stucco work adorns this casino.

a different kind of escape: Inspired by Madame de Pompadour (Louis XV's mistress), ladies would hold court with writers, artists, and avant-garde types.

▶ Cross the bridge and continue straight for 100 yards along *Marzaria San Zulian*. On the way, notice the metal, two-foot-high flood barrier braces at shop doors—and how merchandise is elevated in anticipation of high water (local insurance doesn't cover floods).

   When you hit the next schizophrenic Per S. Marco arrow (in front of the church), go right a few steps, then left onto *Marzaria dell'Orologio*, a street named for where you're heading: the Clock Tower. You're approaching St. Mark's Square (back where you started this walk) and the city's front door.

Rialto to Frari Church Walk

Cross the Rialto Bridge, and dive headlong into Venice's thriving market area. The area west of the Grand Canal feels less touristy—a place where more "real" Venetians live. We'll start by exploring a few downhome places near the Rialto, especially the lively produce and stinky fish markets. Then we'll explore the San Polo area, passing everyday shops, pubs, and quiet squares that are at least a bit off the tourist path. We'll end at the Frari Church and nearby Scuola San Rocco—a delightful artistic dessert.

ORIENTATION

Length of This Walk: Allow a leisurely hour.

When to Go: The markets are lively only in the morning. The produce market is closed on Sunday, and the fish market is closed on Sunday and Monday.

Church of San Polo: €3, Mon-Sat 10:30-13:30 & 14:30-17:00, closed Sun.

Tragicomica Mask Shop: Mon-Sat 10:00-13:00 & 14:00-19:00, on Calle dei Nomboli at #2800, +39 041 721 102, www.tragicomica.it. The owners are generally happy to show their workshop on weekdays to customers who buy a mask, though it's best to make a reservation.

THE WALK BEGINS

Starting atop the Rialto Bridge, gaze down the bridge (away from the St. Mark's side). This area is where Venice got its start centuries ago as a global commercial power, and today it still houses the city's main market. Behind the tourist-trinket stands are still real jewelry shops with a long tradition.

▶ *Head down the bridge and start up the street. About 50 yards onward, you'll see an old square on your right. Go to its fountain.*

❶ Campo San Giacomo

This square, named for the church that faces it, was ground zero for Venice's lively global trade in the 1500s. As ships docked near Rialto Bridge and unloaded their goods, this courtyard became the center of trade and banking. Traders needed bankers, so this square also became Venice's "Wall Street." The line of buildings on the long side of the courtyard (now restaurants) was once a strip of banks. It's still called *Bancogiro,* which means "the place where merchants banked." Today, these popular eateries are worth checking out.

Opposite the church, find the granite statue of a hunchback supporting steps leading to a column. Back when this neighborhood was the Wall Street of medieval Europe, this column was the closest thing they had to a *Wall Street Journal.* Someone climbed the stair each noon and stood on the column to read aloud the daily news from the doge: which ships had docked, the price of pepper, and so on.

The church facade is one of the oldest in town. The spirit of St.

Cross the Rialto Bridge into less-touristed Venice.

Campo San Giacomo, near the Rialto Market

James the Minor, for whom the church is named, watched over the business community, encouraging honesty in a time when banking regulations were nonexistent. Today the church's tranquil interior hosts an exhibition of historical musical instruments (free).

▶ *Facing the church, turn left and walk between the Bancogiro buildings to the edge of the Grand Canal.*

❷ Historic Docks

Back when the Rialto Bridge was still a drawbridge (until the 1590s), big ships docked right here to load and unload their spices, oil, wine, and jewels. They'd exchange money and goods at the Bancogiro banks. The large white building nearby was and still is the city's fiscal administration building. Notice how it tilts out (probably because the bridge's huge foundation is compressing the mud beneath it).

Now walk toward the Rialto Bridge along the canal to a little canalside dead-end. Take in the great view of the bridge. The big building directly across the Grand Canal—originally used by German merchants for lodging and trade (see the "Germanicus" seal)—is now a shopping center popular for its roof terrace view.

You're standing under a former prison. Study the iron grills over the windows. Notice the interlocking pipes with alternating joints—you couldn't cut just one to escape.

▶ *From the prison, walk back along the canal and through the triple archway. You'll reach the stands (in Casaria square) of Venice's...*

❸ Produce Market *(Erberia)*

Colorful stalls offer fresh fruit and vegetables, some quite exotic. Nothing is grown on the island of Venice, so everything is shipped in

Rialto to Frari Church Walk

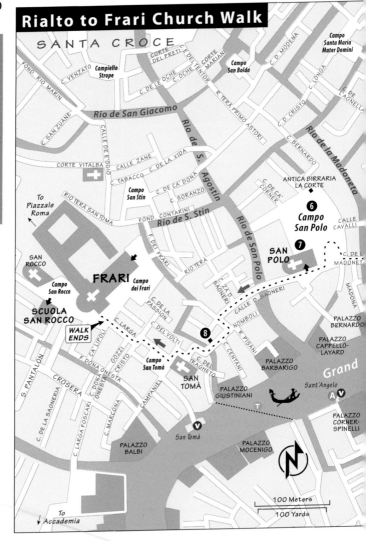

SANTA CROCE

FOND. RIO MARIN

C. VENZATO

Campiello Strope

C. DE LE OCHE

C. DE LE OCHE

CORTE DEL PRETI

F. DEI TENTOR

CORTE DEI MARIANI

Campo San Boldo

C. D. MODENA

Campo Santa Maria Mater Domini

C. LONGA

C. DE L'AGNELLA

Rio de San Giacomo

C. SAN ZUANE

CALLE DE L'OGIO

R. TERÀ PRIMO ASTORI

C. D. CRISTO

C. BERNARDO

Rio de la Madoneta

CORTE VITALBA

CALLE ZANE

C. TABACCO

C. DE LA VIDA

Rio de S. Agostin

ANTICA BIRRARIA LA CORTE

C. DE CA' CORNER

To Piazzale Roma

RIO TERÀ SANT'OMÀ

Campo San Stin

C. DE CA' DONA

C. SORANZO

FOND CONTARINI

Rio de S. Stin

6

Campo San Polo

CALLE CAVALLI

SAN ROCCO

RIO TERÀ

F. DEI FRARI

RIO TERÀ

Rio de San Polo

SAN POLO

7

C. DE I MADONET

Campo San Rocco

FRARI

Campo dei Frari

C. DE LA PASSION

C. DE LA SAONERI

CALLE D. SAONERI

NOMBOLI

R. PISANI

MADONA

SCUOLA SAN ROCCO

C. LARGA

C. DEL VOLTI

WALK ENDS

CA' LIPOLI

GOZZI

C. DEL TRAGHETO

Campo San Tomà

8

C. CENTANI

PALAZZO BERNARDO

PALAZZO CAPPELLO-LAYARD

PALAZZO BARBARIGO

S. PANTALON

CROSERA

F. DONA ONESTA

F. DONA ONESTA

CRISTO

C. MARCONA

CAMPANIEL

SAN TOMÀ

PALAZZO GIUSTINIANI

Grand

Sant'Angelo

A Ⓥ

C. DE LA SAONERIA

C. LARGA FOSCARI

San Tomà

Ⓥ

T

PALAZZO MOCENIGO

PALAZZO CORNER-SPINELLI

PALAZZO BALBI

Ⓝ

To Accademia

100 Meters

100 Yards

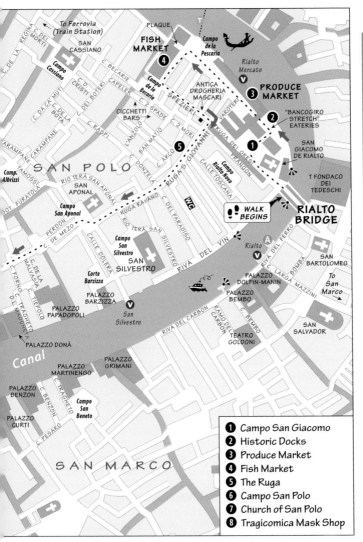

To Ferrovia (Train Station)

PLAQUE

FISH MARKET

SAN CASSIANO

Campo Cassiano

C. DE LA REGINA

C. DEI MORTI

Campo de la Pescaria

Rialto Mercato

PRODUCE MARKET

ANTICA DROGHERIA MASCARI

Campo de le Becarie

C. BECARIE

C. CAFELER

SPEZIERI

C. DRISTI

PALAZZO

C. DEI BOTERI

C. DA CA MUTI

C. DELA BOTA

CICCHETTI BARS

C. RASPI

C. 2 SPADE

C. 2 MORI

LANZOLO

SAN MATIO

C. DONZELA

RUGA DEL ORESI

VAROTERI

FRANCON

"BANCOGIRO STRETCH" EATERIES

SAN GIACOMO DE RIALTO

T FONDACO DEI TEDESCHI

ARAMPANE CARAMPANE

SAN POLO

Camp. Albrizzi

SOT. FURATOLA

C. ARCO

Campo Rialto Novo

RUGA DI S. GIOVANNI

CALLE TOSCANA

RIO TERA SAN APONAL

SAN APONAL

Campo San Aponal

PERDON

RUGA RAVANO

C. DEL PARADISO

WC

WALK BEGINS

RIALTO BRIDGE

C. DE MEZO

CALLE DOLERA

RIO TERA SAN SILVESTRO

Campo San Silvestro

SAN SILVESTRO

RIVA DEL VIN

Rialto

RIVA DEL FERRO

C. LARGA MAZZINI

SAN BARTOLOMEO

To San Marco

Corte Barzizza

PALAZZO BOMBA

PALAZZO DOLFIN-MANIN

PALAZZO BEMBO

C. BEMBO

PALAZZO BARZIZZA

San Silvestro

RIVA DEL CARBON

RAMO DEL CARBON

TEATRO GOLDONI

SAN SALVADOR

PALAZZO PAPADOPOLI

C. DE LA MALVASIA

C. FORNO C. TIEPOLO

D. I. MADONETA

C. FORNO C. TRAGHETO

PALAZZO DONÀ

Canal

PALAZZO MARTINENGO

PALAZZO GRIMANI

PALAZZO BENZON

C. BENZON

Campo San Beneto

PALAZZO CURTI

C. PESARO

C. TRAGHETO

SAN MARCO

1. Campo San Giacomo
2. Historic Docks
3. Produce Market
4. Fish Market
5. The Ruga
6. Campo San Polo
7. Church of San Polo
8. Tragicomica Mask Shop

Many Venetians shop daily at the *Erberia*.

The Ruga cuts through the San Polo area.

daily from the mainland. The Rialto Mercato vaporetto stop is a convenient place for boats to unload their wares. With the city's narrow streets, everything must be hand-hauled on dollies by hardworking stevedores and deliverymen. At #203 (halfway down the first set of stalls, on the left), the shop called Macelleria Equina sells horse (*cavallo*) and donkey (*asino*) meat. Continue along the canal, exploring the produce stalls.

▶ *Follow your nose straight ahead until you enter the brick open-air arcade that houses the fish market. Turn left and explore your way through the other arcade, as well.*

❹ Fish Market (*Pescaria*)

This market is especially vibrant and colorful in the morning. The open-air stalls have the catch of the day—Venice's culinary specialty. Find eels, scallops, crustaceans with five-inch antennae, and squid soaking in their own ink—all destined for tonight's risotto. This is the Venice that has existed for centuries: Workers toss boxes of fish from delivery boats while shoppers step from the *traghetto* (gondola shuttle) into the action. Customers are exacting and expect to know whether the fish is fresh or frozen, farmed or wild, Atlantic or Mediterranean (look for labels at some stands). Local fish are small and considered particularly tasty because of the high concentration of salt at this end of the Adriatic. Any salmon you see are farmed, mostly from northern Europe. It's not unusual to pay €30 per kilo (about 2.2 pounds) for the best fish.

In the courtyard between the two market buildings, find the plaque on the wall that lists the minimum length a fish must be for it to be sold. Sardines must be seven centimeters; *peocio* (mussels) must be three centimeters. (Below that, someone has added a penis joke.)

▶ *Continue exploring the market while walking away from the water. You emerge on **Campo de la Becarie** ("Butchers Square"). Turn left and follow Ruga dei Spezieri ("Spicers Road") for about 100 yards. Along the way, pop into Antica Drogheria Mascari (on the right at #380), a small storefront that hides a vast enoteca with 600 different Italian wines, spices, and gifty edibles. Thirty yards past the drogheria, turn right. You're at the head of a major street, called Ruga Vechia San Giovanni.*

❺ The Ruga

This busy street is lined with shops that Venetians patronize for their basic goods. It gets progressively less touristy and more practical the farther you go. There are fewer trinkets and more clothes, bread, shoes, blenders, shampoo, and underwear.

Note that the second street you pass on the right, Sotoportego dei Do Mori, leads to several recommended *cicchetti* bars serving the Venetian version of tapas (see the Eating chapter).

▶ *At this point, you can pretty much put this book down and walk for a while, checking out the scene. Walk up the Ruga, which changes names as you go. Just keep heading basically straight. When in doubt, follow signs pointing to Ferrovia (train station). Our next stop is just a few minutes away—the vast, hard-to-miss square called...*

❻ Campo San Polo

One of the largest squares in Venice, Campo San Polo is shaped like an amphitheater, with its church tucked away in the corner (just ahead of you). Antica Birraria la Corte, a fine and family-friendly pizzeria/*ristorante,* is located at the far side (see page 179). The square's amphitheater shape was determined by a curved canal at the base of the buildings on the right. Today, the former canal is now a *rio terà*—a street made of landfill.

▶ *On the square is the...*

❼ Church of San Polo (S. Paolo Apostolo)

This church, one of the oldest in Venice, dates from the ninth century (English description at ticket desk). The wooden, boat-shaped ceiling recalls the earliest basilicas built after Rome's fall. While the church is skippable for many, art enthusiasts visit to see Tintoretto's *Last Supper*

Tintoretto's *Last Supper*—one of the less-touristed versions of this scene found in Venice

(near the entrance) and Giovanni Battista Tiepolo's *Virgin Appearing to St. John of Nepomuk* (middle of the long wall).

The highlight here is a series of dramatic paintings by Tiepolo's son Domenico—*The Stations of the Cross.* Spend some time following the stations, then find Domenico's happy ending on the ceiling—the Resurrection, with Jesus springing from the tomb.

▶ *From the Church of San Polo, continue about 200 yards (following Ferrovia signs). Along the narrow alley called Calle dei Nomboli, on the right at #2800, is...*

❽ Tragicomica Mask Shop

One of Venice's best mask stores, Tragicomica is also a workshop that offers a glimpse into the process of mask making. Venice's masks have always been a central feature of the celebration of Carnevale—the local pre-Lent, Mardi Gras-like blowout. You'll see Walter, Alessandra, and Giuliana hard at work.

Many masks are patterned after standard characters of the theater style known as commedia dell'arte: the famous trickster Harlequin, the beautiful and cunning Columbina, the country bumpkin Pulcinella (who later evolved into the wife-beating Punch of marionette shows), and the solemn, long-nosed Doctor (*dottore*).

▶ *Continuing along, cross the bridge and veer right. You'll soon see purple signs directing you to Scuola Grande di San Rocco. Follow these until you bump into the back end of the Frari Church (with Scuola San Rocco next door). If you're looking for perhaps the best Venetian art in situ, you've found it. (See the 📖 Frari Church Tour chapter.)*

St. Mark's to San Zaccaria Walk

San Zaccaria, one of the oldest churches in Venice, is just a few minutes on foot from St. Mark's Square. The church features a Bellini altarpiece and a mysterious submerged crypt that might be the oldest place in Venice. This short, easy-to-follow walk gets you away from the bustle of St. Mark's, includes a stroll along the waterfront, and brings you right back to where you started.

ORIENTATION

Length of This Walk: Allow about an hour for a leisurely walk and stop inside the church (though the actual distance is short).

Church of San Zaccaria: Free, €3 to enter crypt and choir chapel, €1 coin to illuminate Bellini's altarpiece, Mon-Sat 10:00-12:00 & 16:00-18:00, Sun 16:00-18:00 only. Mass is held daily at 18:30 and Sun also at 10:00 and 12:00.

THE WALK BEGINS

❶ Piazzetta dei Leoni

Facing St. Mark's Basilica, start in the small square to the left of the church (Piazzetta dei Leoni), with the 18th-century stone lions that kids love to play on. See the well and those drains in the pavement (behind the lions)? The felines are sitting on a cistern, fed by four drains.

Notice the nicely restored north side of the basilica, with fine 14th-century reliefs. Notice also the prayer entrance below the exquisite Porta dei Fiori. To the left, behind a black metal fence, is the tomb of Daniele Manin, the great 19th-century Italian and Venetian patriot.

The big white building at the far end of the square houses the offices of Venice's "patriarch," the special title given to St. Mark's bishop. Venice's most famous patriarch went on to be Pope John XXIII, the popular "Sixties Pope," who oversaw major reforms in the Catholic Church (Vatican II). Locals still refer to him as "Il Papa Buono" (the good pope). A plaque on the building calls him "Beato Giovanni XXIII," and in 2013, Pope Francis made him a saint.

The lions of Piazzetta dei Leoni

Bridge of Sighs—and bridge of sightseers

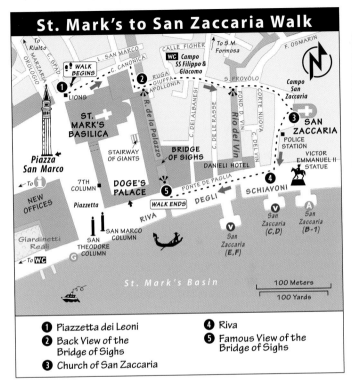

St. Mark's to San Zaccaria Walk

1 Piazzetta dei Leoni
2 Back View of the Bridge of Sighs
3 Church of San Zaccaria
4 Riva
5 Famous View of the Bridge of Sighs

▶ *Head east along Calle de la Canonica, past a fine English-language bookstore, then turn right and circle behind the basilica. Passing some of the sexiest gondoliers in town, you'll reach a bridge (Ponte Selfie Stick) with a...*

❷ Back View of the Bridge of Sighs

This lesser-known view of the Bridge of Sighs also lets you see the tourists who are ogling it, their cameras cocked. You can just see the Lady Justice relief (centered above the windows), with her sword and scales—a reminder that the courts were to the right and the prison to the left.

On the basilica side of the bridge is a common sight in neighborhood Venice: a streetside altarpiece and a donation box. As the street signs tell you, the bridge you're on marks the boundary between two traditional neighborhoods, the *sestiere* (district) of San Marco and that of Castello.

▶ *Continue east, passing through a lively, small square. Notice the two archaic relics of bygone days—an old well and a newspaper stand. You'll cross another bridge with a view of a "Modern Bridge of Sighs," which connects two wings of the exclusive Danieli Hotel. Continue east another 50 yards, through the Gothic gate of what was once a cloistered Benedictine convent, and into a square where you see the...*

❸ Church of San Zaccaria

Back in the ninth century—when Venice was just a collection of wooden houses and before there was a St. Mark's Basilica—a stone church and monastery stood here. Today's structure dates mostly from the 15th century.

The tall facade designed by Mauro Codussi (who also created the Clock Tower in St. Mark's Square) and others is early Renaissance. The "vertical" effect produced by the four support pillars that rise up to an arched crown is tempered by the horizontal, many-layered stories and curved shoulders.

In the northwest corner of Campo San Zaccaria (near where you entered) is a weathered plaque from 1620 listing all the things that were prohibited "in this square" (*in questo campo*), including games, obscenities, dishonesty, and robbery, all "under grave penalty" (*sotto gravis pene*).

▶ *Enter the church. The second altar on the right holds the...*

Body of Zechariah (S. Zaccaria)

Of the two bodies interred above the altar, the lower one in the glass case is the reputed body of the church's namesake—Zechariah, the father of John the Baptist. Back when mortal remains were venerated and thought to bring miracles to the faithful, Venice was proud to own the bones of St. Zechariah ("San Zaccaria," also known as Zacharias).

▶ *The church is blessed with fine art. On the opposite side of the nave (second altar on the left), you'll find...*

Bellini's *Madonna* sits in a fake niche that appears to be an extension of the church.

Giovanni Bellini, *Madonna and Child with Saints* (*Sacra Conversazione*), 1505

Mary and the baby, under a pavilion, are surrounded by various saints interacting in a so-called *sacra conversazione* (holy conversation), which in this painting is more like a quiet meditation. The saints' mood is melancholy, portrayed with lidded eyes and downturned faces. A violinist angel plays a sad solo at Mary's feet.

This is one of the last of Bellini's paintings in the *sacra conversazione* formula, the newer type of altarpiece that liberated the Virgin, Child, and saints from the separate cells of the older triptych style. Compare this to his other variations on this theme in the Accademia and Frari Church. The life-size saints stand in an imaginary niche in the church wall—the pavilion's painted columns match those of the real church. We see a glimpse of trees and a cloudy sky beyond. Bellini establishes a 3-D effect using floor tiles. The four saints pose symmetrically, and there's a harmony in the big blocks of richly colored robes—blue, green, red, white, and yellow. A cool white light envelops the whole scene, creating a holy ambience. (To add even more light, drop a €1 coin in the box in front of the altar.)

The ever-innovative Bellini was productive until the end of his long life—he painted this masterpiece at age 75. The German artist Albrecht Dürer said of him: "He is very old, and still he is the best painter of them all."

▶ *On the right-hand side of the nave is the entrance to the...*

Crypt

Before you descend into the crypt, pause in the first room (Chapel of Sant'Atanasio) to study **Tintoretto's *Birth of John the Baptist*** (c. 1560s, on the altar), which tells the back story of Zechariah. In the background, old Zechariah's wife, Elizabeth, props herself up in bed while nurses hold and coo over her newborn son, little John the Baptist. The birth was a miracle, as she was past childbearing age. On the far right, old bearded Zechariah—the star of this church—witnesses the heavens opening up, bringing this miracle to Earth.

The five **gold thrones** (displayed in this room or one of the next rooms) were once seats for doges. Every Easter, the current doge would walk from St. Mark's Square to this religious center and thank the nuns of San Zaccaria for giving the land for the square.

The small next room contains religious objects as well as an engraving of the doge parading into Campo San Zaccaria.

Next comes the **Chapel of San Tarasio,** dominated by an impressive 15th-century prickly gold altarpiece by Antonio Vivarini. The predella (seven small scenes beneath the altarpiece) may be by Paolo Veneziano, the 14th-century grandfather of Venetian painting. Look down through glass in the floor to see the 12th-century mosaic floor from the original church. In fact, these rooms were parts of the earlier churches.

Finally, go down the nearby staircase to the **crypt**—the foundation of a church built in the 10th century. The crypt is low and the water table high, so the room is often flooded, submerging the bases of the columns. An old stone altar topped with a Virgin statue heightens the mystery...calling up echoes of the Dark Ages.

▶ *Emerge from the Church of San Zaccaria back into the small campo. Before leaving the campo, check out the small (free) art gallery tucked behind the trees, the thirst-quenching water fountain, and the pink*

Carabinieri police station (a former monastery), marked by the Italian flag. Then exit the square at the far end, and head south until you pop out at the waterfront, right on the...

❹ Riva

The waterfront promenade known as the Riva was built not for tourists but as part of the port of San Marco. Until recently, big ships tied up here. Today it's home to some of the town's finest and most famous hotels—and provides a great view of the Church of San Giorgio Maggiore (one stop away on vaporetto #2).

Before turning right, look left. The big equestrian monument depicts **Victor Emmanuel II,** who helped lead Italy to unification and became the country's first king in 1861. Beyond that (over the bridge) is the four-columned **La Pietà Church,** where Antonio Vivaldi once directed the music. Five bridges farther along (not visible from here) are the Arsenale and Naval History Museum (described in the Sights chapter).

For a peek at the *most* famous and luxurious hotel, turn right, cross over one bridge, and nip into the **Danieli Hotel.** Tuck in your shirt, stand tall and aristocratic, and (with all the confidence of a paying guest) be swept by the revolving door into the sumptuous interior of what was once the Gothic Palazzo Dandolo. As was the design of Venetian *palazzi*, the ground floor was originally a warehouse, with the offices and living quarters upstairs. While you check out the Danieli's restaurant menu (that's why you're there, isn't it?), admire the lobby, the old-style chandeliers, the water-taxi drive-up entrance, and the occasional celebrity. Since 1820, the Neo-Gothic Danieli has

San Zaccaria crypt is often flooded.

Grand hotels along the Riva promenade

been Venice's most exclusive hotel. Exquisite as all this is, it still gets flooded routinely in the winter.

▶ *Facing the water, turn right and head west toward St. Mark's Square. The commotion atop a little bridge marks the...*

❺ Famous View of the Bridge of Sighs

The Bridge of Sighs connects the Doge's Palace (left) with the doge's prison (right). The bridge let justice be very swift indeed, as convicted criminals could, upon sentencing, be escorted directly from the palace's secretive courtroom to prison without being seen in public.

Notice the beefy bars on the prison. There were no windows, so throughout the year it would alternate between very hot and very cold. The top floor, below the lead roof, was nicknamed "The Oven." While designed for 300 people, the prison routinely held 500.

From this historic bridge (according to romantic legend), prisoners took one last look at Venice before entering the dark and unpleasant prison. And sighed. Lord Byron picked up on the legend in the early 1800s and gave the bridge its famous nickname, making this sad little span a big stop on the Grand Tour. Look high up on your left—although that rogue Casanova wrote of the bridge in his memoirs, he was actually imprisoned here in the Doge's Palace. Check out the carved relief on the palace corner, to your left, showing the biblical scene of drunken Noah spilling his wine.

Nowadays, while the bridge is a human traffic jam of gawking tourists during the day, it remains breathtakingly romantic in the lonely late-night hours.

▶ *Your tour's over, and the place where you started is just around the corner. (By the way, if you need some quick cash, this is a great place to pick a pocket. There's lots of bumping, and everyone's distracted....)*

Sights

Venice's greatest sight is the city itself. As well as seeing world-class museums and buildings, make time to wander narrow lanes, linger over a meal, or enjoy evening magic on St. Mark's Square. One of Venice's most delightful experiences—a gondola ride, worth ▲▲▲—is covered in the Activities chapter.

When you see a 📖 in a listing, it means the sight is described in greater detail in a self-guided walk or tour in this book. A 🎧 means the walk or tour is also available as a free audio tour (via my Rick Steves Audio Europe app—see page 11). Some walks and tours are available in both formats—take your pick. This is why some of Venice's most important sights get the least coverage in this chapter—we'll explore them in greater depth elsewhere in this book.

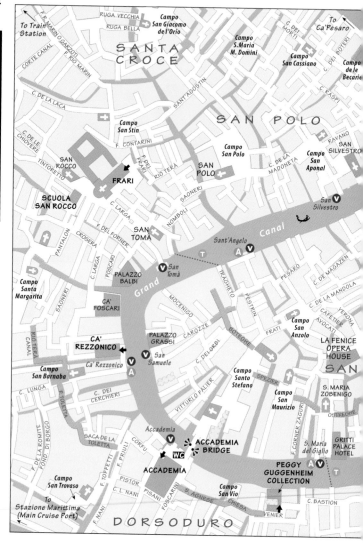

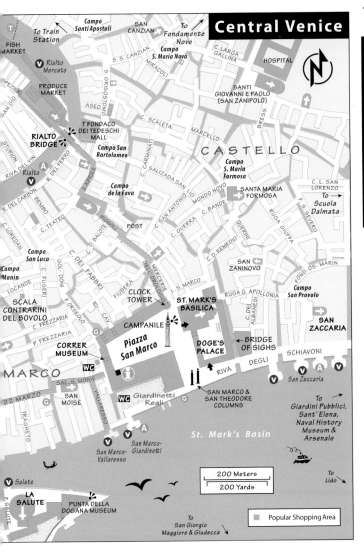

FISH MARKET

To Train Station

Campo Santi Apostoli

SAN CANZIAN

To Fondamente Nove

S. S. CANZIAN

Campo S. Maria Nova

C. LARGA GALLINA

HOSPITAL

Rialto Mercato

MIRACOLI

SPEZIERI

PRODUCE MARKET

S. GRIGOSTOMO

C. SCALETA

SANTI GIOVANNI E PAOLO (SAN ZANIPOLO)

SAN GIO.

ASEO

T FONDACO DEI TEDESCHI MALL

MARCELLO

C A S T E L L O

RIALTO BRIDGE

Campo San Bartolomeo

C. CARMINATI

SALIZADA SAN LIO

Campo S. Maria Formosa

C. L. SAN LORENZO

STURION

Rialto

R. DEL FERRO

2 APRILE

Campo de la Fava

MONDO NOVO

SANTA MARIA FORMOSA

To Scuola Dalmata

RIVA DEL VIN

R. DEL CARBON

BEMBO

PIGNOLI

C. SAN ANTONIO LIO

C. BANDE

RUGA GIUFFA

F. S. SEVERO

POST

C. GUERRA

QUERINI

Campo San Luca

C. TEATRO

C. D. BALOTE

MERCERIE DELL'OROLOGIO

C. D. REMEDIO

FOND. OS. MARIN

Campo Manin

GOL. DONI

C. DEI FABBRI

FIUBERA

L. S. MARCO

SAN ZANINOVO

RUGA G. APOLLONIA

Campo San Provolo

LOCANDE

C. FUSERI

F. FORSEOLO

CLOCK TOWER

ST. MARK'S BASILICA

C. DEI ALBANESI

SCALA CONTRARINI DEL BOVOLO

C. FREZZARIA

P. FREZZARIA

CAMPANILE

DOGE'S PALACE

BRIDGE OF SIGHS

SAN ZACCARIA

CORRER MUSEUM

G

Piazza San Marco

WC

RIVA

DEGLI

SCHIAVONI

San Zaccaria

M A R C O

SAL. S. MOISE

VALLARESSO

WC

Giardinetti Reali

G

SAN MARCO & SAN THEODORE COLUMNS

22 MARZO

SAN MOISE

TRAGHETO

St. Mark's Basin

To Giardini Pubblici, Sant' Elena, Naval History Museum & Arsenale

San Marco-Vallaresso

San Marco-Giardinetti

Salute

To Lido

LA SALUTE

PUNTA DELLA DOGANA MUSEUM

To San Giorgio Maggiore & Giudecca

200 Meters
200 Yards

Popular Shopping Area

SIGHTSEEING STRATEGIES

Avoiding Lines and Crowds

Venice is inundated with day-trippers from the mainland, and cruise-ship passengers from 10:00 to about 16:00. Major sights are busiest in the late morning, making this a smart time to explore the back lanes. Sights that have crowd problems get even more packed when it rains.

Three sights are often plagued by long lines: **Saint Mark's Basilica,** the **Doge's Palace,** and the **Campanile** bell tower—and the only way to be sure to avoid a wait is to book a timed-entry ticket online in advance. You may also save time by booking ahead for the Accademia. For the rest of Venice's sights, you should be fine just dropping by at any time.

If you didn't plan ahead, and are confronted by a long line for the Doge's Palace, purchase your ticket at the Correr Museum across St. Mark's Square. And for the Campanile bell tower, remember that you can skip it entirely if you're going to the similar San Giorgio Maggiore bell tower—which actually offers a better view.

Sightseeing Passes and Discounts

Venice offers a dizzying array of combo-tickets and sightseeing passes. Note that many of the most visit-worthy sights in town (the Accademia, Peggy Guggenheim Collection, Scuola San Rocco, Campanile, and St. Mark's Basilica—and its sights within that charge admission) are not covered by any basic pass.

Museum Pass: Busy sightseers may find value in this pass, which covers the **Doge's Palace, Correr Museum, Ca' Rezzonico** (Museum of 18th-Century Venice), **Ca' Pesaro** (modern art), the **Glass Museum** on the island of Murano, and the **Lace Museum** on the island of Burano. At €35 (€18 for youth and seniors), this pass is an obvious value if you plan to see the Doge's Palace, Correr Museum, and one or two of the other covered museums. Buy it at any participating museum or via their websites (www.visitmuve.it).

SAN MARCO

Venice's historic heart stretches north from St. Mark's Square to the Rialto Bridge, east to the Church of San Zaccaria, and west to La Fenice Opera House. The handiest vaporetto stops are San Marco-Vallaresso (100 yards west of the square) and the four docks of San Zaccaria (150 yards east of the square).

This area can be very crowded at midday (10:00-17:00), so try to do your sightseeing here early or late. It's another world altogether at night—lantern-lit magic under a ceiling of stars.

Use two of my walks to lace together sights in this area:

　📖 St. Mark's to Rialto Loop Walk
　📖 St. Mark's to San Zaccaria Walk

▲▲▲St. Mark's Square (Piazza San Marco)

This grand square is surrounded by splashy, historic buildings and music-filled cafés. By day it's a world of pigeons and tourists. By night it's your private rendezvous with the romantic Venetian past.

　📖 See the St. Mark's Square Tour chapter.

Sightseeing in the St. Mark's Square area is especially crowded at midday.

▲▲▲ St. Mark's Basilica (Basilica di San Marco)

This one-of-a-kind church is adorned with Byzantine-style domes outside and gold mosaics inside. St. Mark's bones lie under the altar. Three separate museums in the church show off rare treasures, a Golden Altarpiece, and the four bronze horse statues.

   📖 See the St. Mark's Basilica Tour chapter.

▲▲▲ Doge's Palace (Palazzo Ducale)

The seat of the Venetian government and home of its ruling duke, or doge, this was the most powerful half-acre in Europe for 400 years. Walk through once-lavish (now sparse) rooms wallpapered by great Venetian painters, learn about Venetian government, and finish by crossing the Bridge of Sighs into the notorious prison.

   📖 See the Doge's Palace Tour chapter.

▲ Bridge of Sighs

This much-photographed bridge connects the Doge's Palace with the prison. Supposedly, a condemned man would cross this bridge, take one last look at the glory of Venice, and sigh. Though overhyped, the Bridge of Sighs is undeniably tingle-worthy, especially after dark.

   For more on the bridge, see the 📖 St. Mark's to San Zaccaria Walk chapter and the 📖 Doge's Palace Tour chapter.

▲▲ Correr Museum (Museo Correr)

This uncrowded museum gives you a good overview of Venetian history and art. The doge memorabilia, armor, banners, statues (by Canova), and paintings (by Titian, Veronese, the Bellini family and others) re-create the festive days of the Venetian Republic. And it's all accompanied—throughout the museum—by good English descriptions and views of St. Mark's Square.

You'll enter the museum through the long loggia overlooking the square. The first few rooms (Rooms 4-6) highlight Venice's greatest homegrown sculptor, Antonio Canova (1757-1822). He created high-polished, slender, beautiful figures—often arranged in groups that are interesting from many angles—and combined the cool lines of classicism with the romantic sentiment of Venice. In *Orpheus and Eurydice* (1776), the Greek poet is leading his beloved back from hell when she's suddenly tugged backward. Orpheus smacks his forehead in horror, but he must continue on, leaving an empty space between them.

Correr Museum—First Floor

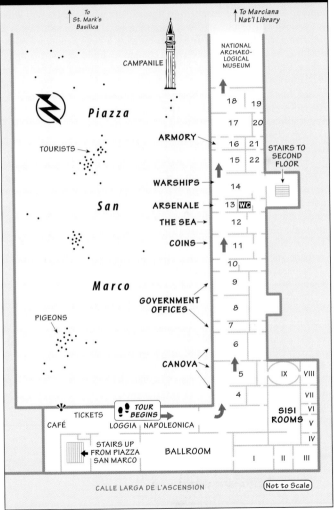

To St. Mark's Basilica

To Marciana Nat'l Library

NATIONAL ARCHAEO-LOGICAL MUSEUM

CAMPANILE

Piazza

TOURISTS

San

Marco

PIGEONS

18 19
17 20
ARMORY → 16 21
15 22

STAIRS TO SECOND FLOOR

WARSHIPS → 14
ARSENALE → 13 WC
THE SEA → 12
COINS → 11
10
9
GOVERNMENT OFFICES 8
7
6
CANOVA 5 IX VIII
4 VII

SISI ROOMS VI
V

TICKETS

TOUR BEGINS →

CAFÉ LOGGIA NAPOLEONICA

STAIRS UP FROM PIAZZA SAN MARCO

BALLROOM IV

I II III

CALLE LARGA DE L'ASCENSION Not to Scale

If you're fascinated by opulent rooms reflecting the eclectic tastes of 19th-century aristocrats, take a quick detour into the nearby "Sisi Rooms." Otherwise, continue into Rooms 7-10, where you'll find what was once the government offices. Here the world of the doges comes to life with portraits of them and other bigwigs, a doge's cap, rare books in walnut bookcases, and a Murano chandelier under a wood-beamed ceiling. Room 11 has a Venetian ducat—99 percent pure gold—that was once Europe's strongest currency. Rooms 12-15 focus on Venice and the sea. Look for models of the sleek, oar- and wind-powered warships that ruled the waves. Find the various sketches that depict the city's famed shipbuilding center—the Arsenale, which could crank out a galley a day. Rooms 16-18—the Armory—display everything from swords and pikes to early guns.

Next, walk through the National Archaeological Museum (so-so classical statues) until you enter the impressive **Marciana National Library,** two rooms with masterful artwork. On the reading-room ceiling are 21 *tondi* (round paintings)—some by Paolo Veronese—illustrating the virtues needed to overcome possible roadblocks to learning. Look for the bare-breasted figure of Lust being driven away by Madam Diligence. In the classroom, artists painted the ceiling with a trompe l'oeil effect that makes the room appear even higher than it is. The painting in the center, by Titian, shows Lady Wisdom seated in the clouds as she contemplates her reality in a mirror.

The second floor traces Venetian painting from golden Byzantine icons to Florentine-inspired 3-D to Venice's trademark soft-focus beauty. Room 36 highlights the family that single-handedly brought Venetian painting into the Renaissance—the Bellinis. The famous Giovanni Bellini (c. 1430-1516) specialized in forever-young, pastel-colored Virgins holding rosy-cheeked Baby Jesuses. Finally, in Room 38, Carpaccio's well-known *Two Venetian Gentlewomen* (c. 1490) are surrounded by exotic pets and amusements, absent-mindedly awaiting their menfolk. Fascinating stuff, but my eyes—like theirs—are starting to glaze over...

▶ *€30 combo-ticket includes Doge's Palace, covered by Museum Pass; daily 10:00-19:00, Nov-March 10:30-17:00; elegant café, enter at far end of square directly opposite basilica, +39 041 240 5211, http://correr. visitmuve.it.*

Clock Tower (Torre dell'Orologio)

Built during the Renaissance in 1496, the Clock Tower marks the entry to the main shopping drag, called the Mercerie, which connects St. Mark's Square with the Rialto Bridge. The bronze men swing their huge clappers at the top of each hour. Notice one of the world's first "digital" clocks on the tower facing the square (with dramatic flips every five minutes). You can go inside the Clock Tower with a prebooked 45-minute guided tour that takes you close to the clock's innards and out to a terrace with good views over the square and city rooftops.

▶ *€13 tour ticket includes admission to the Correr Museum—where the tour starts—as well as the National Archaeological Museum and the Marciana National Library; must reserve ahead—tours in English Mon at 11:00, Tue-Wed at 14:00, Fri and Sun at 11:00 and 14:00; no kids under age 6; +39 041 4273 0892, http://torreorologio.visitmuve.it.*

▲Campanile (Campanile di San Marco)

This dramatic bell tower replaced a shorter tower, part of the original fortress that guarded the entry of the Grand Canal. That tower crumbled into a pile of bricks in 1902, a thousand years after it was built. Ride the elevator 325 feet to the top of the bell tower for one of the best views in Venice (especially at sunset). For an ear-shattering experience, be on top when the bells ring. The golden archangel Gabriel at the top always faces into the wind. Beat the crowds and plan your summit to enjoy the crisp morning air or the cool evening breeze.

▶ *€10 on-site, where you'll wait in line; €12 timed-entry ticket lets you skip the line (buy online in advance or use the posted QR code at the entrance to book on the spot); daily roughly 9:30-20:45, shorter hours off-season; may close during bad weather, www.basilicasanmarco.it.*

For more on the Campanile, 📖 see the St. Mark's Square Tour chapter.

La Fenice Opera House (Gran Teatro alla Fenice)

For 200 years, great operas and famous divas debuted here, in one of Europe's most famous opera houses. In 1996, an arson fire completely gutted the theater. But La Fenice ("The Phoenix") rose from the ashes, thanks to an effort to rebuild the historic landmark. To see the results at their most glorious, attend an evening **performance** (theater box office open daily 10:00-17:00, +39 041 272 2699, www.teatrolafenice.it).

Venice's Best Views

- The soaring Campanile on St. Mark's Square
- The balcony of St. Mark's Basilica
- Rialto Bridge, with a free, expansive view of the Grand Canal (and a cooling breeze)
- The luxury "mall" T Fondaco dei Tedeschi (just north of the Rialto Bridge) with great Grand Canal views
- Accademia Bridge, overlooking the Grand Canal and dome of La Salute Church
- The cupola of La Salute Church
- The Church of San Giorgio Maggiore's bell tower, with views of Venice and all around the lagoon

During the day, you can take an **audioguide tour** of the opera house. All you really see is the theater itself; there's no "backstage" tour of dressing rooms, and the dry 45-minute guide mainly recounts two centuries of construction. But the auditorium is impressive: pastel blue with sparkling gold filigree, muses depicted on the ceiling, and a starburst chandelier.

▶ *€11 audioguide tour (or download their app), generally open daily 9:30-18:00 but can vary—to confirm, check calendar at www.festfenice. com. La Fenice is on Campo San Fantin, between St. Mark's Square and the Accademia Bridge.*

For more on the opera house, see the 📖 St. Mark's to Rialto Loop Walk chapter.

▲Island and Church of San Giorgio Maggiore

This is the dreamy church-topped island you can see from the waterfront by St. Mark's Square. The striking 16th-century church, designed by Andrea Palladio (1508-1580) with his trademark classical touch, features art by Tintoretto, a bell tower, and unforgettable views of Venice.

The church, with a facade like a Greek temple, feels so striking because it just doesn't fit with old-school Venice. Palladio made no concessions to the Byzantine legacy of Venice that you see across the

Two of Venice's best views are from the towers of St. Mark's (left) and San Giorgio (right).

water at the Doge's Palace. His style was hugely influential on generations of architects in England and America.

The interior is white and well lit by clear glass, with a clarity and mathematical perfection that exudes the classical world.

On the wall to the right of the altar is a *Last Supper* (1592-1594) by Tintoretto. The table stretches diagonally away on a tiled floor, drawing us in. The scene is crowded—servants and cats mingle with wispy angels—and a blazing lamp radiates supernatural light. Your eyes go straight to a well-lit Christ, serving his faithful with both hands. In Tintoretto's *Manna from Heaven,* on the opposite wall, hungry Israelites gather God's heaven-sent bread.

Take the elevator up the bell tower for a stunning view. Look north and you'll see Venice's famous skyline. Facing east across the lagoon, find the long, narrow island of Lido. Facing west is the nearby island of Giudecca. The old flour mill at the far end is now a Hilton hotel.

Finally, looking up, you see the bells that chime on the hour and half-hour. You've been warned.

▶ *Church—free, open daily 9:00-19:00, Nov-March 8:30-18:00; bell tower elevator—€8, runs daily 10:00-18:00 (in off-season, may close for lunch 13:00-14:00), does not run during Sun services; +39 041 522 7827.*

To reach the island from St. Mark's Square, take the five-minute ride on vaporetto line #2 from San Zaccaria (runs every 12 minutes from dock B, direction: Piazzale Roma).

DORSODURO

▲▲Accademia (Galleria dell'Accademia)

Venice's top art museum, packed with highlights of the Venetian Renaissance, features paintings by the Bellini family, Titian, Tintoretto, Veronese, Tiepolo, Giorgione, and Canaletto. It's just over the wooden Accademia Bridge from the San Marco action.

Start upstairs in small Room 24 to see Titian's *Presentation of the Virgin* (1534-1538). Titian painted the work especially for this room, fitting it neatly around the door on the right. The door on the left was added later, cutting into Titian's masterpiece. This work is typical of Venetian Renaissance art. Here and throughout this museum, you will find: 1) bright, rich color; 2) big canvases; 3) Renaissance architectural backgrounds; 4) slice-of-life scenes of Venice; and 5) 3-D realism.

Now that we've gotten a taste of Renaissance Venice at its peak, let's backtrack and see art by some of Titian's predecessors. In Room 2, Giovanni Bellini's *Enthroned Madonna with Child* (c. 1480) brings Mary down from her golden heaven into the same spacious, 3-D world we inhabit. Bellini painted creamy complexions with soft outlines, bathed in the "haze" he put over his scenes, giving them an idealized, glowing, serene, and much-copied atmosphere. In Giorgione's *The Tempest* (c. 1505, Room 8), the serenity of this beautiful landscape is about to be shattered by an approaching storm, the center of the composition.

Room 10 features Venetian art at its peak, including an epic Venetian Renaissance canvas. Veronese's enormous *Feast in the House*

Veronese's colorful *Feast in the House of Levi* captures Venice's Renaissance-era joie de vivre.

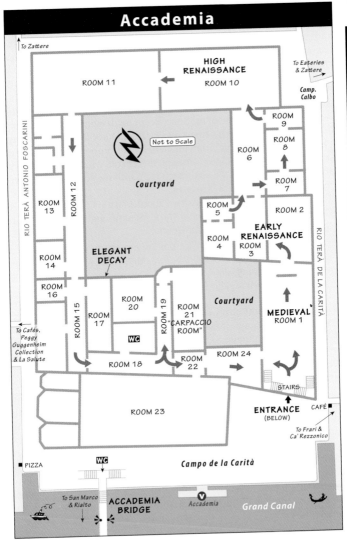

Accademia

To Zattere

HIGH RENAISSANCE
ROOM 10

To Eateries & Zattere

Camp. Calbo

ROOM 11

ROOM 9

ROOM 8

ROOM 6

ROOM 7

Not to Scale

Courtyard

RIO TERÀ ANTONIO FOSCARINI

ROOM 12

ROOM 13

ROOM 5

ROOM 2

EARLY RENAISSANCE

ROOM 4

ROOM 3

ROOM 14

ELEGANT DECAY

ROOM 16

ROOM 15

ROOM 17

ROOM 20

ROOM 19

ROOM 21 "CARPACCIO ROOM"

Courtyard

MEDIEVAL
ROOM 1

RIO TERÀ DE LA CARITÀ

To Cafés, Peggy Guggenheim Collection & La Salute

WC

ROOM 18

ROOM 22

ROOM 24

STAIRS

ENTRANCE (BELOW)

CAFÉ

ROOM 23

To Frari & Ca' Rezzonico

PIZZA

WC

Campo de la Carità

To San Marco & Rialto

ACCADEMIA BRIDGE

V *Accademia*

Grand Canal

of Levi (1573) fills your field of vision with a Venetian party. Everyone's dressed to kill, conversation roars, and the servants bring on the food and drink. The original title was *The Last Supper*, until Veronese was hauled before the Inquisition. Rather than change the painting, he just changed the title.

In Room 11 are two more Venetian masterworks. Look for Titian's *Pietà* (c. 1573), which he painted to hang over his own tomb. The canvas is dark and somber, with rough, messy proto-"Impressionist" brushstrokes. A dramatic line of motion sweeps up diagonally, culminating in Mary Magdalene, who turns away, flinging her arm and howling. The kneeling old man is Titian himself. In Tintoretto's *The Removal of St. Mark's Body* (1562-1566), Venetian merchants whisk away the body of St. Mark, as though we could step right into the scene—or the merchants could carry Mark into ours.

From Room 11, there are two more must-visit spots: Room 20 (Gentile Bellini's *Procession in St. Mark's Square*), and Room 21 (Vittore Carpaccio's *The Legend of Saint Ursula*).

▶ *€12, €14 for timed-entry ticket that allows you to skip the line (buy online in advance); Tue-Sun 8:15-19:15, Mon until 14:00, last entry one hour before closing; dull audioguide—€6, vaporetto: Accademia, +39 041 524 3354, www.gallerieaccademia.it.*

▲▲Peggy Guggenheim Collection

The popular museum of far-out art, housed in the American heiress' former retirement palazzo, offers one of Europe's best reviews of the art of the first half of the 20th century. Visitors get a glimpse into Peggy's fascinating life, her home, and art by artists she knew personally as friend, lover, and patron.

In 1920, young Peggy Guggenheim (1898-1979) traveled to Paris, where she lived a bohemian life with avant-garde artists. She spent the war years in America, where her New York art gallery inspired a generation. In 1948, Peggy moved to Venice, renovating this small palazzo on the Grand Canal. It became a mecca for "Moderns," from composer Igor Stravinsky to actor Marlon Brando to writer Truman Capote to Beatle John Lennon and (Peggy's travel buddy) Yoko Ono.

You'll enter a garden courtyard sprinkled with statues. There's a wing to the left (with the café) and a wing to the right (with the main collection), plus a modern annex. The collection is (very)

Peggy Guggenheim Collection

Grand Canal

TERRACE

LIVING ROOM
ABSTRACT

LIBRARY
ABSTRACT

ANGEL OF THE CITY SCULPTURE

GUEST BEDROOM
SURREALISM

PEGGY'S BEDROOM

PEGEEN

WC

KITCHEN
KANDINSKY

DINING ROOM
CUBISM

ENTRANCE HALL

EAST WING
POLLOCK

Shaded area =
Peggy's Palazzo

SCHULHOF COLLECTION

To Salute

Sculpture Garden

TOUR BEGINS

DOGS' GRAVE

PEGGY'S GRAVE

TICKET CHECK

CALLE SAN CRISTOFORO

MUSEUM CAFÉ

WC

MUSEUM SHOP

WC

LOCKERS/ CLOAK-ROOM

EXIT

TEMPORARY EXHIBITIONS

WC

TICKET DESK

ENTRY

To
Accademia

FONDAMENTA VENIER DEI LEONI

Not to Scale

Rio de le Toresele

roughly chronological, starting with Cubism and ending with post-World War II artists. Start at the far corner of the garden (along a brick wall), where you'll find the grave of Peggy's many long-haired Lhasa Apsos (marked "Here Lie My Beloved Babies"). Peggy's ashes are buried alongside, marked with a simple plaque: "Here Rests Peggy Guggenheim 1898-1979."

In the entrance hall, you can picture Peggy greeting guests—standing before the trembling-leaf mobile by Alexander Calder, flanked by Picasso and Magritte paintings, surrounded by her yapping dogs and meowing cats, and wearing her Calder-designed earrings, Mondrian-print dress, and Catwoman sunglasses.

In the dining room, the skinny table reminds us that this museum was, indeed, her home for the last 30 years of her life. Most of the furniture is now gone, but the walls are decorated much as they were when she lived here, with paintings and statues by her friends, colleagues, and mentors. On the terrace, featuring an exuberant equestrian statue by Marino Marini, you can imagine Peggy sipping coffee while taking in this unbelievable view of the Grand Canal. The bedroom displays the silver headboard by Calder that originally adorned Peggy's bed. Nearby are childlike paintings done by Peggy's daughter, Pegeen.

The collection's strength is its Abstract, Surrealist, and Abstract Expressionist art. Highlights include Picasso's art-shattering Cubist masterpiece, *The Poet*. Picasso's *On the Beach* was Peggy's favorite painting. Marcel Duchamp's *Nude* is a blurred self-portrait of Peggy's mentor. Abstract works by Kandinsky and Mondrian were highly influential on America's young Abstract Expressionists. You'll see Surrealist works by Yves Tanguy (Peggy's boyfriend) and Max Ernst (her husband). In Ernst's *The Antipope*, the horse-headed nude in red is supposedly a portrait of Peggy. Other Surrealist highlights include an ominous suburban scene by Magritte and a photorealistic dreamscape by Dalí. Finally, you'll find work by Jackson Pollock, a.k.a. "Jack the Dripper," who became famous largely thanks to Peggy's support.

▶ *€16, smart to get a timed-entry ticket during busy times; Wed-Mon 10:00-18:00, closed Tue; audioguide—€7, pricey café, vaporetto: Accademia or Salute, +39 041 240 5411, www.guggenheim-venice.it.*

Exuberant modern art at the Guggenheim

La Salute—impressive church, fine art

▲La Salute Church (Santa Maria della Salute)

This impressive church, a prime example of Venetian Baroque, was built and dedicated to the Virgin Mary by grateful survivors of the 1630 plague. Ornate and gleaming white, with a huge, crown-shaped dome, the landmark church dominates the skyline where the Grand Canal meets the lagoon. The dome terrace of La Salute is open to visitors, providing a breathtaking view of the heart of Venice.

The architect, Baldassare Longhena (1598-1682), remade Venice in the Baroque style, and La Salute was his crowning achievement. He sank countless pilings into the sandy soil to help support the mammoth dome.

Inside, the church has a bright, healthy glow, well lit from clear glass windows. The nave is circular, surrounded by chapels. At the main altar, marble statues tell the church's story: The Virgin (center) is approached for help by a kneeling, humble Lady Venice (left). Mary shows compassion and sends an angel baby (right) to drive away Old Lady Plague.

Artwork in the church includes three paintings by Luca Giordano (in the three side chapels to the right of the altar), Titian's *Pentecost* (the chapel to the left of the altar), and works by Tintoretto and Titian in the (not always open) Sacristy.

▸ *Church—free; sacristy—€6; dome terrace—€8; church open daily 9:00-12:00 & 15:00-17:30; winter from 9:30; sacristy open similar but irregular hours Tue-Sun, closed all day Mon and Tue morning; dome open Wed-Sun 10:00-17:00; vaporetto: Salute, +39 041 274 3928, www.basilicasalutevenezia.it/la-basilica.*

▲Punta della Dogana

This museum of contemporary art, housed in the former Customs House at one end of the Grand Canal, features cutting-edge 21st-century art in spacious rooms. This isn't Picasso and Matisse, or even Pollock and Warhol—those guys are ancient history. But if you're into the likes of Jeff Koons, Cy Twombly, Rachel Whiteread, and a host of newer artists, the museum is world class. The displays change completely about every year, drawn from the museum's large collection—so large it also fills Palazzo Grassi, farther up the Grand Canal.

▶ *€20 (varies depending on exhibit); Wed-Mon 10:00-19:00, closed Tue, last entry one hour before closing; small café, near La Salute Church (vaporetto: Salute), +39 199 112 112 within Italy, 041-200-1057 from abroad, www.palazzograssi.it.*

▲▲Ca' Rezzonico (Museum of 18th-Century Venice)

This Grand Canal palazzo offers the most insightful look at the life of Venice's rich and famous in the 1700s. Wander under ceilings by Tiepolo, among furnishings from that most decadent century, enjoying views of the canal and paintings by Guardi, Canaletto, and Longhi.

Start on the first floor, in the 5,600-square-foot Room 2, and imagine a glittering party of masked and powder-wigged dandies, beneath a trompe l'oeil ceiling. Room 3 has the first of several ceiling frescoes by Venice's own G. B. Tiepolo (1696-1770), the renowned decorator of Europe's palaces. Four white horses pull a chariot carrying Rezzonico family newlyweds. Tiepolo's zero-gravity scenes, bright colors, classical motifs, and sheer unbridled imagination made his frescoes blend seamlessly with ornate Rococo furniture. Room 4 has luminous pastel portraits and miniatures by the celebrated Venetian Rosalba Carriera (1675-1757). Room 5 is decorated with Rococo tapestries, a mirror, and a door showing an opium smoker on his own little island paradise. Room 6, the Throne Room, has views over the Grand Canal and a Tiepolo ceiling that blows a hole in the roof, allowing angels to descend to honor old man Rezzonico. As the gang returns to heaven, the lady in blue leaves her leg dangling over the "edge" of the fake oval.

Rooms 7-11 have more period furniture, the carved-wood fantasies of Andrea Brustolon (Room 10), and a sedan chair (Room 11) to transport the rich in red-velvet luxury.

The second floor features paintings. Room 12 has two "postcard" scenes of Venice by Canaletto. With a wide-angle view and photographic clarity, he captures the canals, palaces, and hanging laundry of the city he loved. In Room 13, find scenes (by Tiepolo's son) of the hook-nosed bumpkin Pulcinella partying at Carnevale. Room 15 has a canvas by Guardi where men (wearing the traditional mask, three-cornered hat, and cowl) hit on masked prostitutes. As the 1700s were coming to an end, the decadent gaiety of Venice was giving way to modern democracy and the Industrial Age. Room 16 presents a startling contrast: Tiepolo's lush Rococo fantasy overhead and the straightforward scenes of everyday life by Pietro Longhi (1702-1785).

▶ *€10, €1 fee to reserve online, covered by Museum Pass; Wed-Mon 10:00-18:00, Nov-March until 17:00, closed Tue year-round; ticket office closes one hour before museum, audioguide—€4, café on the Grand Canal, vaporetto: Ca' Rezzonico, +39 041 241 0100, http://carezzonico. visitmuve.it.*

SAN POLO AND SANTA CROCE

▲▲▲Rialto Bridge

One of the world's most famous bridges, this distinctive and dramatic stone structure crosses the Grand Canal with a single confident span. Designed in 1588 by architect Antonio da Ponte, it took only five years to complete. The arcades along the top of the bridge help reinforce the structure...and offer some enjoyable shopping diversions, as does the Rialto Market nearby (produce market closed Sun, fish market closed Sun-Mon).

See the 📖 St. Mark's to Rialto Loop Walk chapter and the 📖 Rialto to Frari Church Walk chapter.

▲T Fondaco dei Tedeschi View Terrace

In the Middle Ages, Venice was the world's trading center, hosting scores of nationalities, each with its own caravanserai-like center. The most famous, just off the Rialto Bridge, was once the home of the Tedeschi (German) traders. Now it's a luxury mall catering to travelers from China and cruise ships, with gourmet food shops, ritzy cafés, and a top-floor terrace offering a unique perspective over the roofs

The upscale T Fondaco dei Tedeschi mall also offers a rooftop view terrace.

of Venice and the Grand Canal. Four times an hour, 70 people are allowed onto the roof for 15 minutes.

▶ *The terrace is free but access requires a reservation (book online at www.dfs.com/en/info/t-fondaco-rooftop-terrace; walk-ins are welcome if there's space, but no guarantees). Terrace open daily 10:30-18:30, June-Aug until 20:15; east side of Rialto Bridge, +39 041 314 2000.*

▲▲Frari Church
(Basilica di Santa Maria Gloriosa dei Frari)
My favorite art experience in Venice is seeing art in the setting for which it was designed—as it is at the Frari Church. It features the work of three great Renaissance masters: Donatello, Giovanni Bellini, and Titian—each showing worshippers the glory of God in human terms.

See the 📖 Frari Church Tour chapter or 🎧 download my free audio tour.

▲▲Scuola San Rocco

Sometimes called "Tintoretto's Sistine Chapel," this lavish meeting hall has some 50 large, colorful Tintoretto paintings plastered to the walls and ceilings.

Start in the ground-floor hall, lined with big, colorful Tintoretto canvases. *The Annunciation* has many typical Tintoretto characteristics: light-dark contrast, twisting, muscular poses, diagonal composition, and rough brushwork. He creates scenes where the miraculous and the everyday mingle side by side.

Upstairs in the Sala dell'Albergo (just off the Chapter Room), follow scenes of Christ's Passion. In *Christ Before Pilate*, Jesus stands literally head and shoulders above his accusers, radiating innocence. The old man in white is Jacopo Tintoretto himself (1518-1594). The drama culminates in the expansive *Crucifixion*. Workers struggle to hoist crosses, mourners swoon, and riffraff gamble for Christ's clothes. Tintoretto focuses all the painting's lines of sight—the ladder on the ground, the angles of the crosses, the sloping hillsides—directly to the center, where Christ rises above it all, crucified but ultimately triumphant.

The huge Chapter Room has 34 enormous oil canvases in gold frames. They tell biblical history—Old Testament on the ceiling, New Testament along the walls—from Adam and Eve (at the

Scuola San Rocco is wallpapered with Tintoretto's *Crucifixion* and other Bible-themed works.

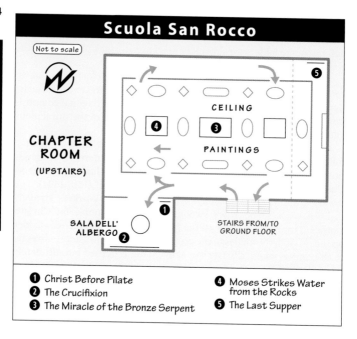

Scuola San Rocco

(Not to scale)

CHAPTER ROOM
(UPSTAIRS)

CEILING

PAINTINGS

SALA DELL' ALBERGO

STAIRS FROM/TO GROUND FLOOR

1 Christ Before Pilate
2 The Crucifixion
3 The Miracle of the Bronze Serpent
4 Moses Strikes Water from the Rocks
5 The Last Supper

Sala dell'Albergo end) to the Ascension of Christ (at the altar end). Tintoretto painted a staggering 8,500 square feet—like covering a house, inside and out, with a tiny artist's brush.

The largest ceiling painting is *The Miracle of the Bronze Serpent.* The half-naked Israelites wrestle with snakes and writhe in pain. At the top of the pile, a young woman gestures toward Moses, who points to a bronze serpent that can heal all who gaze upon it. Walk around beneath the painting and it comes alive like a movie. Tintoretto was the Spielberg of his day, making the supernatural seem tangible. Nearby, in *Moses Strikes Water from the Rocks,* the thirsty Israelites scurry to catch the water, while Moses is the calm center of a wheel of activity.

In *The Last Supper* (on the wall to the left of the altar), a dog, a beggar, and a serving girl dominate the foreground, while the apostles dine in darkness. By emphasizing the ordinary elements, Tintoretto confirmed the faith of the San Rocco brotherhood—that God intervenes miraculously in our everyday lives.

▸ *€10, daily 9:30-17:30, next to the Frari Church (vaporetto: San Tomà), +39 041 523 4864, www.scuolagrandesanrocco.org.*

▲Ca' Pesaro International Gallery of Modern Art

This museum features 19th- and early-20th-century art in a 17th-century canalside palazzo. The collection is strongest on Italian (especially Venetian) artists, but also presents a broad array of other well-known artists. While the Peggy Guggenheim Collection is undisputedly Venice's best modern collection, Ca' Pesaro comes in a clear second—and features a handful of recognizable masterpieces (most notably Klimt's *Judith II,* Kandinsky's *White Zig Zags,* and Chagall's *Rabbi #2*).

▸ *€14, covered by Museum Pass; Tue-Sun 10:00-18:00, Nov-March until 17:00, closed Mon year-round, last entry one hour before closing; close to vaporetto: San Stae, +39 041 721 127, http://capesaro.visitmuve.it.*

CANNAREGIO

Jewish Ghetto

Tucked away in the Cannaregio district is the ghetto where Venice's Jewish population once lived, segregated from the rest of the city. While today's Jewish population is dwindling, the neighborhood still has centuries of history, Jewish-themed sights, and eateries.

In medieval times, Jews were grudgingly allowed to do business in Venice, but they weren't permitted to live here until 1385 (subject to strict laws and special taxes). Anti-Semitic forces tried to oust them from the city, but in 1516, the government compromised by restricting Jews to a special (undesirable) neighborhood. It was located on an easy-to-isolate island near a former foundry (*geto*). In time, the word "ghetto" caught on across Europe as a term for any segregated neighborhood.

Head to Campo de Gheto Novo, the ghetto's center. To reach it from the train station, walk five minutes to the Ponte de Guglie bridge over the Cannaregio Canal. Cross the bridge and turn left. About 50 yards north of the bridge, a small covered alleyway (Sotoportego del Gheto Vechio) leads between the *farmacia* and the Gam-Gam Kosher

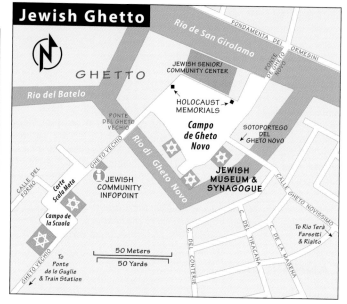

Jewish Ghetto

GHETTO

Rio de San Girolamo

FONDAMENTA DEI ORMESINI

PONTE DE GHETO NOVO

Rio del Batelo

JEWISH SENIOR/ COMMUNITY CENTER

HOLOCAUST MEMORIALS

Campo de Gheto Novo

SOTOPORTEGO DEL GHETO NOVO

PONTE DEL GHETO VECHIO

GHETO VECHIO

Rio di Gheto Novo

JEWISH MUSEUM & SYNAGOGUE

CALLE GHETO NOVISSIMO

CALLE DEL FORNO

Corte Scala Mata

JEWISH COMMUNITY INFOPOINT

Campo de la Scuola

To Rio Terà Farsetti & Rialto

C. DEL TIRACANA

C. DE LA MASENA

C. DEL CONTERIE

GHETO VECHIO

To Ponte de le Guglie & Train Station

50 Meters

50 Yards

Restaurant, through a newer Jewish section, across a second bridge, and into the historic core.

In the 1600s—the Golden Age of Venice's Jews—the Campo had 70 shops, and 5,000 Jews lived nearby, many packed into the six-story "skyscrapers" that still surround the square. To save space, the synagogues were built atop these tenements. The ghetto's two bridges were closed at night. In 1797, Napoleon ended the ghetto's isolation, and in the 1860s, the new Italian state granted Jews full citizenship.

Today the square is quiet. Only a few dozen Jews live in the former ghetto. Look for the large Jewish senior center/community center (Casa Israelitica di Riposo), flanked by two Holocaust memorials. The barbed wire and bronze plaques remind us that it was on this spot that the Nazis rounded up 200 Jews for deportation (only 8 returned). After visiting, exit through Sotoportego del Gheto Novo for the best view of the "fortress ghetto," with tall tenement buildings rising from the canal and an easy-to-lock-up little bridge and gateway.

Bridge to the once-segregated Jewish Ghetto   Calatrava's bridge to the 21st century

SIGHTS

The **Jewish Museum** (Museo Ebraico, may be closed for renovation) is small but well presented. Exhibits include silver menorahs, cloth covers for Torah scrolls, and a concise bilingual exhibit on the Venetian Jewish community.

▸ *Jewish Museum—€10, Sun-Thu 10:30-17:30, Fri until 15:00, Oct-May closes at 17:00, closed Jewish holidays and Sat year-round, modest dress required, small café, temporary office at Calle del Forno 1107, +39 041 715 359, www.museoebraico.it; guided neighborhood tours in English—€12, typically Sun-Fri at 11:00, 12:00, 14:00 and 15:00, no tours Sat and Jewish holidays, reservations.mev@coopculture.it.*

Calatrava Bridge (a.k.a. Ponte della Costituzione)

This controversial bridge, designed by Spanish architect Santiago Calatrava, is just upstream from the train station. Only the fourth bridge to cross the Grand Canal, it carries foot traffic between the train station and bus terminal at Piazzale Roma.

The bridge draws snorts from Venetians. Its construction was expensive (€11 million), the design clashes with the city's medieval and Renaissance architecture, and its orb-shaped carriage (built for wheelchairs) got famously stuck and has since been removed. And, to add practical insult to aesthetic injury, its tempered glass steps—very slippery when wet—are scheduled to be replaced with stone.

CASTELLO

▲Scuola Dalmata di SS Giorgio e Trifone

This little-visited wood-paneled chapel is decorated with the world's best collection of paintings by Vittorio Carpaccio (1465-1526).

The Scuola, a reminder that cosmopolitan Venice was once Europe's trade hub, was one of scores of such community centers for various ethnic, religious, and economic groups, supported by the government partly to keep an eye on foreigners. It was here that the Dalmatians (from a region of Croatia) worshipped in their own way, held neighborhood meetings, and preserved their culture. Your entry fee contributes to one of five such fraternities in Venice still active in this century.

The scenes run clockwise around the room, telling the story of St. George, who slew a dragon and metaphorically conquered paganism.

In the first panel on the far left, George meets the dragon (each day given a sacrificial victim) on the barren plain. George heroically charges forward, and jams his lance through the dragon's skull, to the relief of the damsel in distress (in red). This is one of Carpaccio's masterpieces. In the next panel, George leads the bedraggled dragon (lance still in its head) before the thankful, wealthy pagan king and queen. Next, they kneel before George (now with a red sash, far right) as he holds a pan of water, baptizing them.

The rest of the panels (about St. Jerome and St. Tryphone) are also by Carpaccio. In the last panel on the right, St. Augustine pauses while writing. He hears something. The dog hears it, too. It's the encouraging voice of St. Jerome, echoing mysteriously through the spacious room.

▶ *€6; Tue-Sat 9:30-17:30, Sun 9:30-13:30, Mon 13:30-17:30; reservations may be required—email segreteria@scuoladalmatavenezia.com or check website; on Calle dei Furlani at Castello 3259a, +39 041 522 8828, www.scuoladalmatavenezia.com. The Scuola is located midway between St. Mark's Square and the Arsenale. Go north from Campo San Provolo (by the Church of San Zaccaria), following the street as it changes names from L'Osmarin to St. George to Greci. At the second bridge, turn left on Fondamenta dei Furlani.*

The Arsenale recalls Venice's naval power.

La Biennale's art exhibitions rotate annually.

Naval History Museum, Arsenale, and Ships Pavilion

The mighty Republic of Venice was home to Europe's first great military-industrial complex: a state-of-the-art shipyard that could build a powerful warship of standardized parts in an assembly line (and did so to intimidate visiting heads of state). While the Arsenale shipyard isn't open to the public, you can visit the Naval History Museum and (if it's open) the Ships Pavilion.

The **Naval History Museum** (Museo Storico Navale) features ships and instruments of the republic, including a model of the doge's ornate state barge, gondolas, and Venetian boats of the 19th century. The **Arsenale** is still a military base and is therefore closed to the public, but its massive and evocative gate, the Porta Magna, is worth a look. (To see the gate, turn left as you face the Naval History Museum and follow the canal.) It was one of the first Renaissance structures in Venice. Imagine newly constructed warships parading regally and ominously from the Arsenale down the canal, ready to defend the Venetian Republic. The **Ships Pavilion** (Padiglione delle Navi, across the Arsenale Bridge) shows bigger Venetian boats from the 19th century.

▶ *€10 ticket covers museum and Ships Pavilion; Wed-Mon 11:00-17:00, closed Tue, last entry one hour before closing; off Riva San Biasio, Castello 2148, +39 041 244 1399, www.visitmuve.it/en/museums. From the Doge's Palace, hike six bridges east along the waterfront to the Naval History Museum.*

▲Via Garibaldi: A Neighborhood of Venetians

A 10-minute walk down the Riva from the Doge's Palace, past the Arsenale, is a delightful residential zone around wide Via Garibaldi

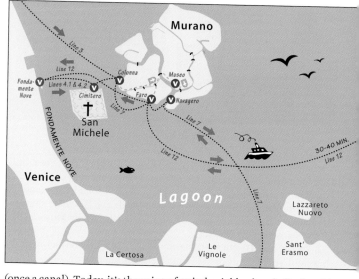

(once a canal). Today, it's the spine of a vital neighborhood—lively with locals, inviting restaurants, and *cicchetti* bars. Stroll the entire length of Via Garibaldi: You'll find real shops rather than souvenir stores, side lanes flanked with laundry flying like flags, children at play, and reasonable prices.

Along the way, you'll pass the grand, gated entry to the Giardino Garibaldi park and find a rare surviving produce boat moored at the end of the street. From the bridge at the end of Via Garibaldi, look left to see the huge walls protecting the massive Arsenale shipyard.

Sant'Elena

Farther from the action and even less touristy is the 100-year-old neighborhood of Sant'Elena, at the far end of the fish's tail, with a kid-friendly park, a few lazy restaurants, and beautiful sunsets over San Marco.

La Biennale

From roughly April through November, Venice hosts an annual art fair—alternating between contemporary art one year and architecture

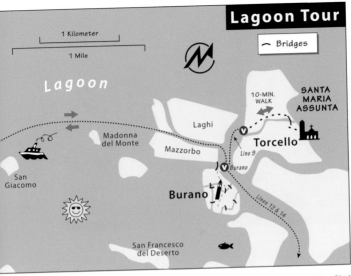

the next—in buildings and pavilions scattered throughout Giardini Pubblici park and the Arsenale (vaporetto: Giardini-Biennale). See the events calendar at www.labiennale.org).

VENICE'S LAGOON

With more time, venture to some nearby islands in Venice's lagoon. While still touristy, they offer an escape from the crowds, a chance to get out on a boat, and some enjoyable diversions for fans of glassmaking, lace, and sunbathing.

Lagoon Tour

Cradled by the lagoon, north of the city, are four islands easily laced together in a pleasant day trip. Here they are, from nearest to farthest.

San Michele (a.k.a. Cimitero) is the cemetery island—the final resting place of Venetians and a few foreign VIPs, from poet Ezra Pound to composer Igor Stravinsky.

▲**Murano,** famous for its glassmaking, is home to several glass

The island of Burano in the lagoon is a smaller, sleepier version of Venice.

factories and the inviting ▲ Glass Museum (€10, covered by Museum Pass, open daily, +39 041 739 586, http://museovetro.visitmuve.it).

▲**Burano's** claim to fame is lacemaking with countless lace shops and a Lace Museum (€5, covered by Museum Pass; closed Mon year-round, +39 041 730 034, http://museomerletto.visitmuve.it). The town itself is a delightful pastel fishing village.

▲**Torcello,** population 20, features Venice's oldest church—Santa Maria Assunta—with impressive mosaics, a climbable bell tower, and a modest museum with sculpture and manuscripts (church-€6, museum-€4; church open daily, museum closed Mon; museum +39 041 730 761).

Here's a plan for linking the islands: Start from St. Mark's Square, the train or bus station, or the Fondamente Nove vaporetto stop. Take the #4.1 or #4.2 vaporetto for Murano. On the way, get off at the Cimitero stop on San Michele to see the cemetery. Continue on to Murano, arriving at the Murano-Colonna stop. Sightsee Murano, as you make your way to the Murano-Faro stop, where you board vaporetto #12 for the trip to Burano (30-40 minutes). From Burano, you can side-trip to Torcello (on the #9). To return to Venice from Burano, take vaporetto #12 all the way back to Fondamente Nove (45 minutes).

For a longer, more scenic return past even more lagoon islands, take the #14 from Burano to the San Zaccaria dock near St. Mark's Square (70 minutes).

Lido Beaches

Venice's nearest beaches are at the Lido, across the lagoon on an island connected to the mainland (which means car traffic). The sandy beachfront is a mix of beach clubs and free-to-enter expanses of sand. At most places, you can rent an umbrella and lounge chair, buy beach gear, get food, or have a drink (vaporetto: Lido S.M.E., walk 10 minutes on Gran Viale S. Maria Elisabetta to beach entry).

Activities

Venice's maze of streets and canals can keep you busy for days. This chapter offers suggestions for tours, shopping, and entertainment.

To get acquainted with the island, consider lacing together Venice's sights with the help of a group walking tour or private guide. Window shop through the glitzy boutiques, dodge the tacky souvenir stands, and treat yourself to fine Venetian glass and lace.

When the sun goes down, a cool breeze blows in from the lagoon, the lanterns come on, the peeling plaster glows in the moonlight, and Venice becomes Europe's most romantic city. Dance to the orchestra music that echoes throughout St. Mark's Square, glide through the sparkling black canals on a romantic gondola, or attend a Vivaldi concert in one of Venice's elegant Baroque venues.

TOURS

🎧 To sightsee on your own, download my series of **free audio tours** that illuminate some of Venice's top sights and neighborhoods (see the sidebar on page 11).

Avventure Bellissime Venice Tours

This company offers several small-group, English-only tours, including a basic two-hour St. Mark's Square introduction and other specialty itineraries (RS%—10 percent discount, €39-55, contact them before booking for a promo code; +39 041 970 499, www.tours-italy.com, info@tours-italy.com).

Alessandro's Classic Venice Bars Backstreets Tours

Alessandro Schezzini organizes two-hour Venetian bar tours (€40/person, most nights at 17:30) that include sampling *cicchetti* snacks with wines at three *bacari* bars. Tours depart almost daily in season when six or more sign up. (Book via email, alessandro@schezzini.it, or by phone at +39 335 530 9024; www.schezzini.it.)

Venicescapes

Michael Broderick's private, themed tours of Venice are intellectually demanding and engrossing for history buffs (various 4- to 6-hour itineraries, 2 people-€280-320 or the USD equivalent, €60/person after that, admissions and transport extra, +39 041 850 5742, mobile +39 349 479 7406, www.venicescapes.org, info@venicescapes.org).

Local Guides

Plenty of licensed, trained guides are available (figure on €75/hour with a 2-hour minimum):

Walks Inside Venice is enthusiastic about teaching (€280/3 hours per group of up to 6, RS%; Roberta: +39 347 253 0560; Sara: +39 335 522 9714; www.walksinsidevenice.com, info@walksinsidevenice.com).

Informative and reliable **Elisabetta Morelli and Corine Govi** run **2Guides4Venice** (Elisabetta: +39 328 753 5220, elisabettamorelli61@gmail.com; Corine: +39 347 966 8346, corinegovi@gmail.com; www.2guides4venice.com).

Venice with a Guide, a co-op of eight good Venetian guides, offers a range of tours (€75/hour, www.venicewithaguide.com).

BestVeniceGuides.it offers a smartly organized online catalog of about 100 local guides (family-friendly guides, shared group tours available, most guides about €75/hour, www.bestveniceguides.it).

Tour Leader Venice specializes in getting you outside of Venice by car or minivan to countryside destinations and the Dolomites—but also offers guided walks in Venice (mobile +39 348 900 0700 or +39 333 411 2840, www.tourleadervenice.com, info@tourleadervenice.com; Igor).

SHOPPING

The merchants of Venice are abundant, making this a fun city for window-shoppers. Trinket stands tuck themselves between internationally famous designer stores and hole-in-the-wall artisan workshops. Anything not made locally is brought in by boat—and therefore generally more expensive than elsewhere in Italy. If you're buying at a market, bargain—it's accepted and almost expected. In shops, you may save by offering to pay cash.

For a private tour focusing on shopping and crafts, contact **Walks Inside Venice,** which offers several itineraries (www.walksinsidevenice.com).

Shopping Neighborhoods
St. Mark's Square and Nearby: The streets closest to St. Mark's Square, and those along the Mercerie (the route between St. Mark's

Sample traditional *cicchetti* on a food tour.

Buy an ornate mask from an artisanal shop.

and the Rialto Bridge), are the most trafficked, with the highest rents and prices in town.

West of St. Mark's, toward the Accademia Bridge, is more elegant and exclusive, with high-fashion shops along Calle Vallaresso.

As you get closer to the Accademia Bridge (around Campo Santo Stefano and Salizzada San Samuele), you'll find more character-istic and affordable stores, such as textile shops, art boutiques, and galleries.

Dorsoduro: The area immediately around the Accademia and Peggy Guggenheim Collection is touristy but does have some worth-while places selling glass art and jewelry. In the opposite direction, a 10-minute walk past the Accademia, is Campo San Barnaba, a lower-rent neighborhood that attracts innovative, less-established artisans.

Rialto Bridge and Nearby: Many of the products here are ed-ible, but there are lots of hole-in-the-wall jewelry and trinket stores on the bridge, under the arcades to the north, and on the Ruga (the street running from the Rialto toward Campo San Polo and the Frari Church). Near the east end of the Rialto Bridge is the luxury shopping mall T Fondaco dei Tedeschi.

What to Buy

Venice has more than its share of ticky-tacky souvenir stores hawking goofy knickknacks and knock-off glassware. But artisanal shops with genuine Murano glass, Burano lace, and Carnevale masks have a long history in the city, and the determined shopper can seek out the real thing. If you press beyond the crowded alleyways around San Marco, you'll discover many small, authentic boutiques and perhaps meet the designers behind the wares.

Glass: Some visitors feel that because they're in Venice, they ought to grab the opportunity to buy glass. Remember that you can buy fine glass back home, too—and under less time pressure.

It's important to be an educated shopper if you are interested in buying glass. Avoid the cheap glass you'll see in touristy shops: Most of it is imported from China or Mexico. Genuine, high-end Venetian glass comes with the signature of the artist etched directly into the glass, along with a number if it's a limited edition piece (for example, 14/30—number 14 of a total of 30 pieces made).

Shops will ship your purchase home for you, but you're likely to pay as much or more for shipping as you are for the item(s), and you may have to pay duty on larger purchases. Make sure the shop insures its merchandise.

If you're serious about glass, visit the island of **Murano,** its glass museum, and its many shops—you'll find greater variety on the island (see page 151).

Masks: In the 1700s, when Venice was Europe's party town, masks were popular to preserve the anonymity of visiting nobles doing things forbidden back home. The tradition continues today at Carnevale. Masks are made of papier-mâché, formed on a clay mold from layers of paper and glue.

Mask shops are all over town. Good ones include **Ca' del Sol,** (near the Church of San Zaccaria on Fondamenta de l'Osmarin at #4964); **Marega Renzo Atelier** (a few steps farther along at #4976A); **Papier Mâché** (near Campo Santa Maria Formosa, at the end of Calle Lunga Santa Maria Formosa, Castello 5174b); **Tragicomica** (near the Frari Church on Calle dei Nomboli at #2800); and **Ca' Macana** (near Campo San Barnaba, Dorsoduro 3172).

Lace: Venice is particularly known for "needle lace," with intricate flowers, leaves, and curling stems, which was used for cuffs, gowns, and frilly collars. On the island of Burano, you'll find many shops such as **Merletti d'Arte dalla Lidia** and the **Lace Museum.** Today, much of the lace is machine-made, but Burano residents cherish the traditional art form and are attempting to revive it, producing tablecloths, doilies, handkerchiefs, and clothing. In Venice, the **Il Merletto** shop just off St. Mark's Square sells pieces crafted by students of the Scuola dei Merletti, the local lace-making school in Burano (San Marco 95).

VAT and Customs

Getting a VAT Refund: If you purchase more than €155 worth of goods at a single store, you may be eligible to get a refund of the 22 percent Value-Added Tax (VAT). Get more details from your merchant or see RickSteves.com/vat.

Customs for American Shoppers: You can take home $800 worth of items per person duty-free, once every 31 days. You can bring in one liter of alcohol duty-free. For details on allowable goods, customs rules, and duty rates, visit Help.cbp/gov.

ENTERTAINMENT AND NIGHTLIFE

You must experience Venice after dark. The city is quiet at night, as the masses of day-trippers return to their mainland hotels and cruise ships.

Evenings here are made for wandering. Enjoy the orchestras on St. Mark's Square. Experience Vivaldi's *Four Seasons* in a candlelit 17th-century church. Pop into small bars for an appetizer and a drink. Lick gelato. As during the day, the city itself is the star.

Gondola Rides

Two hundred years ago, there were 10,000 gondolas that ferried aristocrats through Venice's watery "streets." Today, there are about 400 gondolas in service, used only for tourists. Riding a gondola is simple, expensive, and one of the great experiences in Europe. While this is a rip-off for some, it's a traditional must for romantics.

The price for a gondola starts at €80 for a 30-minute ride during the day. You can divide the cost—and the romance—among up to five people per boat, but only two get the love seat. Prices jump to €100 after 19:00—when it's most romantic and relaxing. Adding a singer and an accordionist will cost an additional €120. Routes are a loop, and gondoliers generally charge extra to drop you any place other than where you started.

Dozens of gondola stations are set up along canals all over town. Establish the price, route, and duration of the trip before boarding, and pay only when you're finished. While prices are pretty firm, you might find them softer during the day. Most gondoliers honor the official prices, but a few might try to scam you out of some extra euros, particularly by insisting on a tip. (While not required or even expected, if your gondolier does the full 30 minutes and entertains you en route, a 5-10 percent tip is appreciated; if he's surly or rushes through the trip, skip it.)

If you've hired musicians and want to hear a Venetian song (*un canto Veneziano*), try requesting "Venezia La Luna e Tu." For cheap water thrills during the day, stick to the one-minute shuttle ride on a Grand Canal *traghetto*. At night, vaporetti are nearly empty, and it's a great time to cruise the Grand Canal on the slow boat #1 (labeled *N* after 23:30).

Hiring a gondolier can be worth the splurge.   Catch an orchestra performance at Caffè Florian.

St. Mark's Square

For tourists, St. Mark's Square is a highlight at night, with lantern light and live music echoing from the cafés. Just being here after dark is a thrill, as **dueling café orchestras** entertain. The ultimate Venetian music scene is at the venerable Caffè Florian. But Gran Caffè Chioggia (facing the Doge's Palace) doesn't charge extra for music and has good jazz nightly. Hang out for free behind the tables (allowing you to move easily on to the next orchestra), or spring for a seat and enjoy a fun and gorgeously set concert. If you sit awhile, expect to pay €15 and up (for a drink and the cover charge for music)—money well spent. Dancing on the square is free—and encouraged.

Several venerable cafés and bars on the square serve expensive drinks outside but cheap drinks inside at the bar. The scene in a bar like **Gran Caffè Lavena** can be great. It's far cheaper to get a drink at any of the hole-in-the-wall bars just off St. Mark's Square; you can get a bottle of beer or even prosecco to-go in a plastic cup.

Wherever you end up, streetlamp halos, live music, floodlit history, and a ceiling of stars make St. Mark's magic at midnight.

Music

For about €30, you can take your pick of traditional Vivaldi concerts in churches throughout town. Most shows start at 20:30 and generally last 1.5 hours. Tickets can usually be bought the same day as the concert.

The **Interpreti Veneziani orchestra,** considered the best group in town, generally performs 1.5-hour concerts nightly at 21:00 inside the sumptuous San Vidal Church (€36, church ticket booth open daily

9:30-21:00 or buy online, north end of Accademia Bridge, +39 041 277 0561, www.interpreteveneziani.com).

Venice's most famous theaters are **La Fenice** (grand old opera house, box office +39 041 2424, see page 100), **Teatro Goldoni** (mostly Italian live theater), and **Teatro Fondamenta Nuove** (theater, music, and dance).

Musica a Palazzo is a unique evening of opera across three rooms at a Venetian palace on the Grand Canal (€85, nightly at 20:30, Palazzo Barbarigo Minotto, Fondamenta Duodo o Barbarigo, vaporetto: Santa Maria del Giglio, San Marco 2504, +39 340 971 7272, www.musicapalazzo.com).

Pubs, Clubs, and Late-Night Spots

There are plenty of zones where people gather to enjoy the late hours. Young Venetians and local night owls congregate in bars near the Rialto Market and along a nearby section of the Grand Canal. A strip of canalside restaurants I've dubbed the "Bancogiro Stretch" is a great place to enjoy a drink and the scene late at night (see page 178). Perhaps the best place to drink beer with an Italian is in an Irish pub—and Venice has several near the Rialto Bridge, including **Devil's Forest Pub** (a block off Campo San Bartolomeo on Calle dei Stagneri at San Marco 5185, +39 041 520 0623, www.devilsforestpub.com) and **Inishark Pub** (closed Mon, on Calle del Mondo Novo, just west of Campo Santa Maria Formosa off Salizada San Lio, at Castello 5787, +39 041 523 5300, www.inisharkpub.com).

In Dorsoduro, a canalfront strip called **Zattere** (near the Zattere vaporetto stop) and the university student zone of **Campo Santa Margarita** (near the Accademia Bridge) are lively nightlife spots. The **Venice Jazz Club** has live music from 21:00 to 23:00 (nightly except Thu and Sun, €20 includes first drink, near Ponte dei Pugni, Dorsoduro 3102, +39 041 523 2056, mobile +39 340 150 4985, www.venicejazzclub.com, Federico).

Sleeping

Choosing the right neighborhood in Venice is as important as choosing the right hotel. For sheer magic, I favor hotels that may be a bit pricier but are close to the action: near St. Mark's Square, the Rialto Bridge, and the Accademia Bridge (in Dorsoduro). I also list a few hotels near the train station (less charming but handy for train travelers). I like places that are clean, central, relatively quiet at night (except for the singing of gondoliers), reasonably priced, friendly, small enough to have a hands-on owner or manager, and run with a respect for Italian traditions.

Venice Hotels

The double rooms in Venice listed in this book range from about €90 (very simple, toilet and shower down the hall) to €400 (plush Grand Canal views and maximum plumbing), with most clustered around €140-180 (with private bathrooms).

Most hotel rooms have a TV and free Wi-Fi, which can vary in strength and quality. Simpler places rarely have a room phone. Pricier hotels usually come with a small fridge stocked with beverages. In Venice, a canalside room sounds romantic, but in reality you might be sleeping next to a busy, noisy, boat- and gondola-clogged "street." The quietest Venetian rooms will probably face a courtyard. As many hotels in central Venice are in historic buildings, rooms tend to be small and stairs are often plentiful. Many do not have an elevator.

Italian hotels typically include breakfast in their room prices. If breakfast is optional, you may want to skip it. While convenient, it's usually pricey for what you get: a simple continental buffet with (at its most generous) bread, croissants, ham, cheese, yogurt, and unlimited *caffè latte*. Breakfast at the corner café can be much cheaper.

The city of Venice levies a tax on hotel rooms to generate income for infrastructure and restoration projects. This tax is generally not reflected in the price ratings in this book, and some hoteliers might ask you to pay it in cash at checkout. It varies from €1 to €5 per person, per night.

Making Reservations

Reserve your rooms as soon as you've pinned down your travel dates, especially if you'll be traveling during peak season (April-June and Sept-Oct). For family-run hotels, it's generally best to book your room directly via email or phone. If you'd rather book online, reserve directly through the hotel's official website (not a booking website). The hotelier wants to know:

- Type(s) of rooms you want and number of guests
- Number of nights you'll stay
- Arrival and departure dates, written European-style as day/month/year (for example, 18/06/24 or 18 June 2024)
- Special requests (en suite bathroom, cheapest room, twin beds vs. double bed, quiet room)
- Applicable discounts (such as a Rick Steves discount, cash discount, or promotional rate)

Sleep Code

Dollar signs reflect the average price of a standard double room with breakfast in high season.

$$$$	**Splurge:** Most rooms over €170
$$$	**Pricier:** €130-170
$$	**Moderate:** €90-130
$	**Budget:** €50-90
¢	**Backpacker:** Under €50
RS%	**Rick Steves discount**

Unless otherwise noted, credit cards are accepted, hotel staff speak basic English, and free Wi-Fi is available. If the listing includes **RS%**, request a Rick Steves discount.

Most places will request a credit-card number to hold your room. If the hotel's website doesn't have a secure form where you can enter the number directly, share this info via a phone call. Cancellation policies can be strict; read the fine print before you book.

Always call or email to reconfirm your room reservation a few days in advance.

Budget Tips

Comparison-shop by checking prices at several hotels (on each hotel's own website, on a booking site, or by email). For the best deal, contact my family-run accommodations directly on the hotel's website, by email, or by phone. When you book direct, the owner avoids the commission and may be able to offer you a discount. Some hotels extend a discount to those who pay cash or stay longer than three nights.

A short-term rental is a popular alternative, especially if you plan to stay for several nights. You can usually find a rental that's comparable to—and even cheaper than—a hotel room with similar amenities. Plus, you'll get a behind-the-scenes peek into how locals live.

Websites such as Airbnb, FlipKey, Booking.com, and VRBO let you browse a wide range of properties. Rental agencies such as InterhomeUSA.com or RentaVilla.com can provide more personalized service.

NEAR ST. MARK'S SQUARE

Central as can be, near sights, shops, restaurants, and handy vaporetto stop San Zaccaria

$$$$ Hotel Campiello Family-run, once part of a 19th-century convent, tranquil, RS%, air-con, elevator.

On Campiello del Vin at Castello 4647, +39 041 520 5764, www.hcampiello.it

$$$$ Hotel Fontana Behind St. Mark's Square, family-run, RS%, family rooms, breakfast on terrace in good weather, air-con, elevator, closed Jan.

On Campo San Provolo at Castello 4701, +39 041 522 0533, www.hotelfontana.it

$$$$ Hotel la Residenza A grand old palace facing a peaceful square, no elevator, air-con.

On Campo Bandiera e Moro at Castello 3608, +39 041 528 5315, www.venicelaresidenza.com

$$$$ Locanda al Leon Feels like a medieval tower house, conscientiously run, RS%, some view rooms, family rooms, air-con.

On Campo Santi Filippo e Giacomo at Castello 4270, +39 041 277 0393, www.hotelalleon.com

$$ Albergo Doni Along a quiet canal, dark and quiet, family-run, RS%, ceiling fans, a few rooms have air-con, Wi-Fi in common areas.

On Fondamenta del Vin at Castello 4656, +39 348 511 1007, albergodoni@hotmail.it

$$$$ Hotel Orion Welcoming, peaceful, and pricey rooms in the center of the action, no elevator, RS%, air-con.

Calle Spadaria, San Marco 700a, +39 041 522 3053, www.hotelorion.it

$$$ Hotel al Piave Comfortable and cheery, enjoyable neighborhood, RS%, family rooms, narrow stairs, air-con.

On Ruga Giuffa at Castello 4838, +39 041 528 5174, www.hotelalpiave.com

$$$ Locanda Casa Querini Bright rooms on a quiet square, behind St. Mark's, RS%, family rooms, air-con.

On Campo San Zaninovo/Giovanni Novo at Castello 4388, +39 041 241 1294, www.locandaquerini.com

$$$ Locanda Silva Well located, small terrace, simple rooms, RS%, closed Dec-Jan, family rooms, air-con, lots of stairs.

On Fondamenta del Remedio at Castello 4423, +39 041 522 7643, www.locandasilva.it

$$ Corte Campana B&B Three quiet, spacious, characteristic rooms, cash only, 2-3 night minimum, air-con, elevator.

On Calle del Remedio at Castello 4410, +39 041 523 3603, mobile +39 389 272 6500, www.cortecampana.com

$$$ Locanda la Corte Wood-beamed rooms—Venetian-style, courtyard, restaurant, RS%, air-con.

On Calle Bressana at Castello 6317, +39 041 241 1300, www.locandalacorte.it

$$ Alloggi Barbaria, simple, characterless rooms on one floor, residential neighborhood, RS%, limited breakfast, air-con in summer, Wi-Fi in common areas.

On Calle de le Capucine at Castello 6573, +39 041 522 2750, www.alloggibarbaria.it

$$$$ Hotel Flora Formal, grand public spaces, rooms have a homey warmth, garden oasis, air-con, elevator.

On Calle Bergamaschi at San Marco 2283a, +39 041 520 5844, www.hotelflora.it

$$$$ Hotel Bel Sito Old World character, peaceful courtyard, picturesque location, RS%, some view rooms, air-con, elevator.

On Campo Santa Maria Zobenigo/del Giglio at San Marco 2517, +39 041 522 3365, www.hotelbelsitovenezia.it

$$$$ Hotel Mercurio A block from La Fenice Opera House, comfortable rooms, family rooms, air-con, lots of stairs.

On Calle del Fruttariol at San Marco 1848, +39 041 522 0947, www.hotelmercurio.com

NEAR THE RIALTO BRIDGE

Choose the busy east side of the bridge (10-minute walk to St. Mark's) or the less-touristy west side; good vaporetto connections

$$$$ Hotel al Ponte Antico Exquisite, professional, plush rooms, terrace overlooks the Grand Canal and Rialto Bridge, air-con.

About 100 yards from Rialto Bridge on Calle dell'Aseo, Cannaregio 5768, +39 041 241 1944, www.alponteantico.com

$$$ Pensione Guerrato Above Rialto produce market, 800-year-old building, charming rooms, RS%, air-con.

On Calle drio la Scimia, San Polo 240a, +39 041 528 5927, www.hotelguerrato.com

$$$ Hotel al Ponte Mocenigo Off the beaten path, great value, 16th-century Venetian palazzo, tranquil rooms, RS%, air-con.

On Salizada San Stae, Santa Croce 1985, +39 041 524 4797, www.alpontemocenigo.com

NEAR THE ACCADEMIA BRIDGE

Quiet ambience of Dorsoduro neighborhood, art galleries, convenient vaporetto stops (Accademia or Zattere)

$$$$ Pensione Accademia Fills 17th-century Villa Maravege, elegant rooms, grand public spaces, air-con, no elevator.

On Fondamenta Bollani at Dorsoduro 1058, +39 041 521 0188, www.pensioneaccademia.it

$$$$ Hotel la Calcina Professional yet intimate, peaceful waterside setting, air-con, no elevator and lots of stairs, rooftop terrace.

At south end of Rio de San Vio at Dorsoduro 780, +39 041 520 6466, www.lacalcina.com

$$$$ Hotel Galleria Old-fashioned and velvety rooms, half with views of the Grand Canal, breakfast voucher for café downstairs, ceiling fans.

On Rio Terà A. Foscarini at Dorsoduro 878a, +39 041 523 2489, www.hotelgalleria.it

$$$$ Hotel Belle Arti Serious staff, grand entry, inviting garden terrace, heavily decorated rooms, air-con, elevator.

On Rio Terà A. Foscarini at Dorsoduro 912a, +39 041 522 6230, www.hotelbellearti.com

$$$$ Don Orione Religious Guest House In an old monastery, classy, peaceful, beautifully located, profits go to mission work in the developing world, air-con, elevator.

On Rio Terà A. Foscarini, Dorsoduro 909a, +39 041 522 4077, www.donorione-venezia.it

$$$$ Ca' San Trovaso Six pleasant rooms, peaceful location, RS%, some view rooms, breakfast voucher for nearby café, tiny roof terrace.

Off Fondamenta de le Romite at Dorsoduro 1350, +39 041 241 2215, mobile +39 349 125 3890, www.casantrovaso.com

$$ Casa di Sara Colorfully decorated, in a leafy courtyard, four quiet rooms, tiny roof terrace, air-con.

Along Fondamenta de le Romite at Dorsoduro 1330, +39 342 596 3563, www.casadisara.com

$$$$ Novecento Hotel Plush rooms, welcoming lounge, breakfast garden, nicely situated, air-con, lots of stairs.

On Calle del Dose at San Marco 2684, +39 041 241 3765, www.novecento.biz

$$$$ Foresteria Levi Comfortable and spacious rooms—some are loft quads, a good deal for families, air-con, elevator.

On Calle Giustinian at San Marco 2893, +39 041 277 0542, www.foresterialevi.it

$$$$ Domus Ciliota Well run, well located, church-owned, peaceful courtyard, half the rooms are used by students during the school year, air-con, elevator.

Off Campo Santo Stefano at Calle delle Muneghe, San Marco 2976, +39 041 520 4888, www.ciliota.it

---

$$$ Hotel San Samuele Tidy rooms in an old residence, great locale, RS%, no breakfast, fans, plenty of stairs.

On Salizada San Samuele at San Marco 3358, +39 041 520 5165, www.hotelsansamuele.com

---

NEAR THE TRAIN STATION

The area lacks charm, but if you must stay here, these places fit the bill.

$$$$ Hotel Abbazia In a former abbey, garden, fun-loving staff, RS%, air-con, no elevator, some ground-floor rooms.

On Calle Priuli dei Cavaletti, Cannaregio 68, +39 041 717 333, www.abbaziahotel.com

---

$$ Hotel S. Lucia Modern and sterile, spacious rooms and tight showers, garden, cheaper rooms with shared bath, air-con, closed Nov-Feb.

On Calle de la Misericordia at Cannaregio 358, +39 041 715 180, www.hotelslucia.com

---

$ Hotel Rossi Sits quietly on dead-end street, well-worn rooms, budget-minded will find it tolerable, air-con, lots of stairs.

On Calle de le Procuratie, Cannaregio 262, +39 041 715 164, hotelrossi.venezia@gmail.com

---

$$$ Albergo Marin Nice but sloppily kept rooms, quiet, residential, air-con.

On Ramo de le Chioverete at Santa Croce 670b, +39 041 718 022, www.albergomarin.it

---

$$ Hotel ai Tolentini Seven rooms on two floors, narrow stairs, above a restaurant, no breakfast, air-con.

On Calle Amai at Santa Croce 197g, +39 041 275 9140, www.albergoaitolentini.it

Eating

The hard fact is that Venice is slowly becoming one big tourist attraction, making it harder and harder to find places with both soul and ethics. For a special meal, savvy travelers will venture far away from the center to distant corners of the lagoon.

Having said that, there are still good places, and (just like Disneyland) you have plenty of choices. The best values are no secret, so if you have your heart set on a particular place, make a reservation.

I list a full range of restaurants and eateries—from budget options for a quick bite to multicourse splurges with maximum ambience. I prefer mom-and-pop, personality-driven places, offering fine value and high quality with a local reputation.

When in Venice...

In general, Italians start their day with a light breakfast (*prima colazione;* coffee—usually cappuccino or espresso—and a pastry, often eaten while standing at a counter). Lunch (*pranzo*) was traditionally the largest meal of the day, eaten at home between 13:00 and 15:00. However, as times have changed, so have eating habits. So, while some Italian families still have a big lunch and a small dinner, others do the reverse. Dinner (*cena*) is usually eaten around 20:00 or 21:00 (maybe earlier in winter).

Restaurants

While touristy restaurants are the norm in Venice, you can still make the most of your meal by dining at one of my recommended listings and following these tips. First trick: Walk away from triple-language menus or laminated pictures of food. Second trick: For freshness, eat fish. Many seafood dishes are the catch of the day. Third trick: Eat later. A place may feel touristy at 19:00, but if you come back at 21:00, it can be filled with locals...or, at least, Italian visitors.

A full Italian meal consists of multiple courses: *antipasto* (appetizer), *primo piatto* ("first dish"—pasta, rice, or soup), *secondo piatto* (main course, usually meat or seafood), and *dolce* (dessert).

For most travelers, a complete, multicourse meal is simply too much food—and the euros can add up in a hurry. To avoid overeating (and to stretch your budget), share dishes. A good rule of thumb is for each person to order two courses. For example, a couple can order and share one *antipasto,* one *primo,* one *secondo,* and one dessert; or two *antipasti* and two *primi;* or whatever combination appeals. Small groups can mix *antipasti* and *primi* family-style (skipping *secondi*).

A *menù turistico* is a made-for-tourists plate of Italian clichés for one fixed price. But locals have their own, typically more interesting version, usually called a *prezzo fisso* or sometimes *menù del giorno* (menu of the day). For a smaller appetite, some restaurants serve a *piatto unico,* with smaller portions of each course on one plate (for instance, a meat, starch, and vegetable).

In Venice, only rude waiters rush you. For speedier service, be prepared with your next request whenever a waiter happens to grace your table. You'll have to ask for the bill—mime-scribble on your raised palm or ask, *"Il conto, per favore?"*

Restaurant Code

Dollar signs reflect the cost of a typical main course.

$$$$ **Splurge:** Most main courses over €25

$$$ **Pricier:** €20-25

$$ **Moderate:** €15-20

$ **Budget:** Under €15

Pizza by the slice and other takeaway food is **$**; a basic trattoria or sit-down pizzeria is **$$**; a casual but more upscale restaurant is **$$$**; and a swanky splurge is **$$$$**.

Quick Budget Meals

The keys to eating affordably in Venice are pizza, bars/cafés, self-service cafeterias, and picnics.

Many Italians head to a pizzeria at dinnertime to order a one-person pie. You'll find hole-in-the-wall shops in every neighborhood baking round, family-size pizzas (20 inches) for €8-15, or "normal" ones (12 inches) for €4-8. Some shops sell *pizza rustica*—thick pizza baked in a large rectangular pan and sold by weight. Clearly indicate how much you want: *un etto*—100 grams—is a hot and cheap snack; *due etti*—200 grams—makes a light meal.

An Italian bar isn't so much a tavern as an inexpensive café. These neighborhood hangouts serve coffee, light food, and drinks from the cooler. Most charge extra for table service. For quick meals, bars usually have trays of cheap, premade sandwiches (*panini*, on a baguette; *piadine*, on flatbread; *tramezzini*, on crustless white bread; or *toasts*, on, well, toast). To save time for sightseeing and room for dinner, stop by a bar for a light lunch, such as a ham-and-cheese sandwich—ideally thrown on the grill to heat up.

At many bars, the custom is to first pay the cashier for what you want, then hand the receipt to a barista who serves you. Because Venice has so few public places to sit and relax, it can be worth a few extra euros to enjoy your coffee, sandwich, or gelato while seated in an air-conditioned café.

Another fast and cheap budget option is an Italian variation on the corner deli: a *rosticceria* (cheap food to go such as lasagna, rotisserie chicken, and sides) or a *tavola calda* bar (a point-and-shoot cafeteria with a buffet spread of meat and vegetables). For a healthy light meal, ask for a mixed plate of vegetables with a hunk of mozzarella.

Picnicking saves lots of euros and is a great way to sample regional specialties. Be daring. Try the fresh ricotta, *presto* pesto, shriveled olives, and any regional specialties the locals are excited about. You're legally forbidden from picnicking anywhere on or near St. Mark's Square except for the waterfront Giardinetti Reali. Though it's legal to eat outdoors elsewhere, you may be besieged by pigeons.

Cicchetti Pubs

Unique to Venice, *cicchetti* bars specialize in finger foods and appetizers that combine to make a speedy and tasty meal. *Cicchetti* (the Venetian version of tapas) was designed as a quick meal for working people. The selection and ambience are best on workdays—Monday through Saturday for lunch or early dinner.

While you can order a plate, Venetians prefer going one-by-one... sipping their wine and trying this...then give me one of those...and so on. Try deep-fried mozzarella cheese, gorgonzola, calamari, artichoke hearts, and anything ugly on a toothpick. *Crostini* (small toasted bread with a topping) are popular, as are marinated seafood, olives, and prosciutto with melon. To get a plate of assorted appetizers for €8, ask for "*Un piatto classico di cicchetti misti da €8.*"

For drinks, start with an *aperitivo:* Order a Bellini, a *spritz con Aperol,* or a prosecco, and draw approving looks from the natives. Enjoy the house wines with the food. An *ombra* ("shadow") is a small glass of wine often offered with *cicchetti.* There are usually several fine wines uncorked and available by the glass. A good last drink is *fragolino,* the local sweet wine—*bianco* or *rosso.* It often comes with a little cookie (*biscotto*) for dipping.

Venetian Cuisine

Along with the basic dishes you'll find all over Italy, Venice has its signature specialties—mainly, a wide variety of catch-of-the-day seafood. Venetian cuisine relies heavily on fish, shellfish, risotto, and polenta.

For appetizers, try a marinated seafood assortment (*antipasto di mare*) or asiago cheese. Risotto (rice simmered in broth) and polenta (grilled cornmeal porridge) are more traditional than pasta. Seafood is the classic main dish. The more exotic it is, the more local: fish

(generally smaller varieties like sardines, not salmon or trout), shell-fish, octopus, eel, weird crustaceans, and cuttlefish (*seppia*). Seafood is often sold expensively by the gram—confirm the total price before ordering. On a menu, "X2" means the price per person for a large, two-person dish.

No meal in Italy is complete without wine. Even the basic house wine (*vino da tavola* or *vino della casa*) is fine with a meal. The island of Venice produces no wine, but the mainland Veneto region is known for Soave (crisp white, great with seafood), valpolicella (light fruity red), amarone (very intense red), and prosecco (a dry sparkling wine, easy to drink too much).

Italian coffee is some of the world's best. Even the most basic hole-in-the-wall bar serves quality espresso, macchiatos, and cappuccinos. Popular liqueurs to finish a meal are *amaro* (a bittersweet herbal drink) and anise-flavored Sambuca. Or pick up a cup or cone of gelato at a *gelateria* and stroll the streets with the rest of Venice, enjoying a bit of edible art.

NORTH OF THE RIALTO BRIDGE

These four places are serious restaurants located in Cannaregio. Consider reservations necessary at each (see map, page 183).

(see map, page 183)

1 **$$$ Trattoria da Bepi** Good, traditional Venetian cuisine and the freshest of ingredients, good seating inside and out (Fri-Wed 12:00-15:00 & 19:00-22:00, closed Thu).

On Salizada Pistor, Cannaregio 4550; +39 041 528 5031, www.dabepi.it

2 **$$ Trattoria Ca' d'Oro Alla Vedova** Venerable place respected for its traditional Venetian cuisine, compact yet romantic (Fri-Wed 11:00-14:30 & 18:30-22:30, closed Thu).

Calle del Pistor, Cannaregio 3912; +39 041 528 5324

3 **$$$$ Vini da Gigio** Expensive Venetian menu, elegant mix of traditional and contemporary (Wed-Sun 12:00-14:30 & 19:00-22:30, closed Mon-Tue).

Behind the church on Campo San Felice, Cannaregio 3628a, +39 041 528 5140, www.vinidagigio.com

4 **$$$$ Taverna al Remer** Venetian mixed-fish appetizer plate is a hit, dine by candlelight under brick vaults and old timbers (Wed-Mon 12:00-14:30 & 19:00-22:30, closed Tue).

Near the Church of San Giovanni Crisostomo, Cannaregio 5701; +39 041 52 8789, https://tavernaremer.com

EAST OF THE RIALTO BRIDGE

Twisty lanes between the Rialto Bridge and Campo Santa Maria Formosa (see map, page 183)

(see map, page 183)

5 **$$ Rosticceria Gislon** A *tavola calda* (buffet line of cooked food), salads, fried mozzarella, pastas, seafood, and more (daily 9:00-21:30).

Calle de la Bissa, San Marco 5424a, +39 041 522 3569

6 **$$ *Cicchetti* near Campo San Bartolomeo:** Three fun, tiny *cicchetti* bars clustered within ten yards of one another (all are open daily). Look for Osteria I Rusteghi, Bar SEPA, and Bacarando Bar.

Facing the back of the statue on Campo San Bartolomeo, turn around, walk to the far right-hand corner of the square, and explore the back lanes

7 **$$ Osteria al Portego** Neighborhood eatery near Campo San Lio, bargain-priced house wine, excellent *cicchetti*, reserve ahead if you want a table (daily 11:30-15:00 & 17:30-22:00).

On Calle de la Malvasia at Castello 6015, +39 041 522 9038, www.osteriaalportego.org

EATING

EATING

8 **$$ Osteria da Alberto** Tasty daily specials: seafood, pastas, and a good house wine; dinner reservations smart—request a table in front (daily 12:00-15:00 & 18:30-22:00).

On Calle Larga Giacinto Gallina, Cannaregio 5401; +39 041 523 8153, www.osteriadaalberto.it

RIALTO MARKET AREA

Thriving spot with places to eat and drink, crowded by day, nearly empty early in the evening, and packed with young Venetians and tourists at night (see map, page 183)

9 **$ The "*Cicchetti* Strip"** Classic bars serving delightful munchies (and some meals) two blocks inland from Rialto Market—look for Bar all'Arco, Cantina Do Mori, Osteria ai Storti, and Cantina Do Spade (long hours daily).

Along Sotoportego dei Do Mori and Calle de le Do Spade

10 **$$-$$$ The "Bancogiro Stretch"** Several eateries in an old bank building along the Grand Canal; serving lunch, between-meal bar snacks, dinner, or late drinks with a youthful crowd; great for a spritz and *cicchetti* (long hours daily).

Between Campo San Giacomo and the Grand Canal

11 **$ Al Mercà Bar** Lively crowd, quality wine by the glass and little snacks, no tables and no interior (Mon-Sat 10:00-14:30 & 18:00-21:00, closed Sun).

On Campo Bella Vienna, San Polo 213

12 **$$$ Trattoria alla Madonna** Traditional dishes (mostly seafood), formal waiters, white tablecloths, relaxing old-Venetian atmosphere, fair prices (lunch from 12:00, dinner from 19:00, closed Wed).

On a quiet lane two blocks from Rialto Bridge, Calle della Madonna, San Polo 594, +39 041 522 3824

13 **$$ Ristorante Vini da Pinto** Tourist-friendly, large menu, relaxing outdoor seating; good fixed-price, three-course seafood meal at lunch only (daily 11:00-23:00).

Campo de le Becarie, San Polo 367a, +39 041 522 4599

14 **$$ Osteria al Ponte Storto** Good-value fish dishes, peaceful location, daily specials, reservations smart (Mon-Sat 12:00-15:00 & 18:00-21:45, closed Sun).

Down Calle Bianca from San Aponal Church, San Polo 1278, +39 041 528 2144

⑮ **$$$$ Trattoria Antiche Carampane** Dressy, small, family-run place with a passion for fish, reservations necessary (Tue-Sat 12:45-14:30 & 19:30-22:30, closed Sun-Mon).

Rio Tera delle Carampane, San Polo 1911, +39 041 524 0165, www.antichecarampane.com

⑯ **$$ Antica Birraria la Corte** Huge array of pizza; on cozy, family-filled square (daily 12:00-15:00 & 18:00-22:30).

On Campo San Polo at #2168, +39 041 275 0570

NEAR ST. MARK'S SQUARE

Two serious restaurants and many cheap-and-cheery options convenient to your sightseeing (see map, page 184)

⑰ **$$$$ Ristorante Antica Sacrestia** Classic restaurant, creative fixed-price meals, wonderful pizzas, reservations smart (Tue-Sun 11:30-15:00 & 18:00-23:00, closed Mon).

On Calle Corona, Castello 4463, +39 041 523 0749, www.anticasacrestia.it

⑱ **$$$ Al Giardinetto da Severino Ristorante** Traditional Venetian fare, white tablecloth elegance, garden out back, reservations smart (Fri-Wed 12:00-15:00 & 19:00-22:00, closed Thu).

On Salizada Zorzi, Castello 4928, +39 041 528 5332, www.algiardinetto.it

⑲ **$$ Rossopomodoro Pizzeria** Fun, practical pizzeria, good prices, handy location (long hours daily).

Calle Larga San Marco 404, +39 041 243 8949

⑳ **$$$ L'Ombra del Leone** Big, modern, and classy; outdoor terrace on Grand Canal, try bar menu of salads and sandwiches, restaurant menu is pricey (long hours daily).

Behind San Moisè Church at Sestiere San Marco 1364, +39 041 241 3519

㉑ **$ Birreria Penasa** Fast and practical, cheap toasted sandwiches and beer (daily 7:00-24:00).

Campo Santi Filippo e Giacomo, +39 041 523 7202

㉒ **$$ Aciugheta Pizzeria** Handy for lunch or a casual dinner, pizzas and *cicchetti* (daily 12:00-24:00)

Campo Santi Filippo e Giacomo, +39 041 522 4292

㉓ **$ Birreria Forst** Meaty sandwiches, order at the bar (daily 9:30-23:00).

Halfway down Calle de le Rasse at #4540, +39 041 523 0557

EATING

ACCADEMIA/DORSODURO

Near Accademia Bridge (pretty touristy), Zattere vaporetto (less touristy), and Campo San Barnaba (most charming—see map, page 187)

㉔ **$$ Bar Foscarini** Next to the Accademia Bridge and Galleria, pizzas and *panini*, Grand Canal view, also serves breakfast (daily 8:00-23:00, Nov-April until 20:30).

On Rio Terà A. Foscarini at Dorsoduro 878c, +39 041 522 7281

㉕ **$ Enoteca Cantine del Vino Già Schiavi** Characteristic *cicchetti*-bar ambience, also a wine shop, indoor and outdoor seating, no WC (Mon-Sat 8:30-20:30, closed Sun).

On Fondamenta Nani at Dorsoduro 992, +39 041 523 0034

㉖ **$$$ Al Vecio Marangon Ristorante** Stylish, rustic, *cicchetti*-style dishes and pastas, tight seating, no reservations, arrive early or be prepared to wait (daily 12:00-22:00).

On Calle de la Toletta at Dorsoduro 1210, +39 041 277 8554

㉗ **$$$ Terrazza dei Nobili** Regional specialties (especially fish) and pizza, tolerable prices, seaside seating, formal service (daily 12:00-24:00).

On Fondamenta Zattere at Dorsoduro 924, +39 041 520 6895

㉘ **$$ Pizzeria Oke** Playful, tables on the embankment and sprawling pizza-parlor interior, be careful to understand the bill—dishes presented as free may end up on your check (daily 11:30-23:00).

On Fondamenta Zattere, Dorsoduro 1414, +39 041 520 6601

㉙ **$$ Ristoteca Oniga** Eclectic yet cozy, tables on the square, focuses on fresh fish and other sea creatures, reservations smart (daily 12:00-14:30 & 19:00-22:30).

Campo San Barnaba, Dorsoduro 2852, +39 041 522 4410, www.oniga.it

㉚ **$$ Osteria Enoteca ai Artisti** Quality dishes, sit inside or at canalside tables, good wines by the glass, reservations smart (Tue-Sat 12:45-14:30 & 19:00-22:00, closed Sun-Mon).

Fondamenta de la Toletta, Dorsoduro 1169a, +39 041 523 8944, www.enotecaartisti.com

㉛ **$ Pizzeria al Profeta** Casual, popular with tourists, great pizza, sprawling interior, garden out back (daily 12:00-14:30 & 19:00-22:30).

Long walk down Calle Lunga San Barnaba to #2671, +39 041 523 7466

㉜ **$$ Enoteca e Trattoria la Bitta** Traditional Venetian food but no fish, local ingredients, reservations required (dinner seatings at 19:00 and 21:00, closed Sun).

Off Campo San Barnaba on Calle Lunga San Barnaba, Dorsoduro 2753a, +39 041 523 0531

CANNAREGIO

Residential area northeast of the train station, around the Jewish Ghetto; explore at sunset, then grab a bite (see map, page 188)

㉝ $$$ Osteria L'Orto dei Mori Chic, creative Venetian cuisine, modern interior, tables also on neighborhood square, reservations smart (Wed-Mon 12:30-15:30 & 19:00-24:00, closed Tue).

On Campo dei Mori at Fondamenta dei Mori, Cannaregio 3386; +39 041 524 3677, www.osteriaortodeimori.com

㉞ $$ Osteria ai 40 Ladroni ("The 40 Thieves") Characteristic, unpretentious; choose between canalside, interior, and garden seating (Tue-Sun 12:00-14:30 & 19:00-22:15, closed Mon).

On Fondamenta de la Sensa, Cannaregio 3253, +39 041 715 736

㉟ $$ Osteria Enoteca Timon Relaxing canalside setting, hipster vibe, nice wines, *cicchetti* (open daily).

On Fondamenta Ormesini, Cannaregio 2754, +39 041 524 6066

㊱ $$ Trattoria Al Mariner East of Osteria Timon, rustic interior, canalside tables, local dishes (Mon-Sat 7:00-24:00, closed Sun).

Fondamenta Ormesini, Cannaregio 2679, +39 041 458 7021

㊲ $$ Gam Kosher All-kosher Venetian dishes, canalside seating, vegetarian options (Sun-Thu 12:00-22:00, Fri 12:00-two hours before Shabbat, Sat one hour after Shabbat-23:00).

Underneath the Sotoportego del Gheto Vechio at #1122, +39 366 250 4505

㊳ $$ Pizzeria Vesuvio A neighborhood favorite, classy indoor seating, pleasant tables outside (daily 11:00-23:00 except closed Wed Oct-April).

On Rio Terà Farsetti, Cannaregio 1837, +39 041 268 9258

㊴ $$ Enoteca Cicchetteria Do Colonne Local dive, loyal following, *cicchetti* and sandwiches, no hot food, handy for a drink and a snack (daily 10:00-21:30).

On Rio Terà del Cristo, Cannaregio 1814, +39 041 524 0453

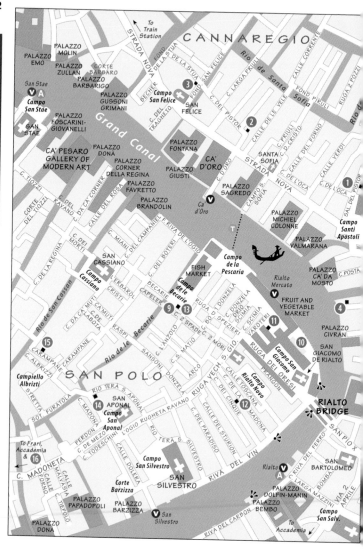

Restaurants near the Rialto Bridge

100 Meters
100 Yards

The "Cicchetti" Strip" & "Bancogiro Stretch"

Aqua Dolce

C. VENIER

To
Vaporetto
Dock

FONDAMENTE NOVE

C. NUOVA

C. DEL FORNO

C. DE LA MADONA

C. PROVERBI

PRETI

CANNAREGIO

Rio dei Mendicanti

FONDAMENTA DEI MENDICANTI

HOSPITAL

Campo de la Cason

C. MAL.

SAN CANZIAN

C. WIDMANN

CALLE DE LA TESTA

Rio de la Panada

SANTI APOSTOLI

Rio dei Santi Apostoli

Campa San Canzian

Campo Santa Maria Novo

❽

CALLE LARGA GALLINA

Campo Corner

RIO TERA

SALIZADA SAN CANZIAN

BOLDÙ

MIRACOLI

SANTA MARIA DEI MIRACOLI

Campo Santi Giovanni & Paolo

SANTI GIOVANNI & PAOLO (SAN ZANIPOLO)

MAGAZEN

BAGATAN

Rio de San Gio Grisostomo

C. CASTELI

C. DE LA ERBE

COLLEONI STATUE

SALIZADA S. ZANIPOLO

SAN GRISOSTOMO

SAN GIOVANNI GRISOSTOMO

C. DE LA ERBE

DONDO

Rio de Santa Marina

C. BRESSANA

MADONA

F. FELZI

ASEO

T FONDACO DEI TEDESCHI

C. SCALETA

FRUTAROL

Campo Santa Marina

C. DEL DOSE

OSTEALEO

BISSA

Campo S. Bartolomeo

❻

PONTE de la FAVA

C. CARMINATI

C. PIOMBO

LARGA

MARCELLO

Rio d. Pestrin

CASTELLO

❶

C. DEL PARADISO

Campo Santa Maria Formosa

C. DEL ORBI

❺

Rio de la Fava

C. DE ANTONIO

SAN LIO

C. DE LA NAVE

SALIZADA SAN LIO

FOND. DEI PRETI

C. LUNGA S. MARIA FORMOSA

SANTA MARIA FORMOSA

C. DE L'AQUILA NERA

C. FAVA

VENIERA

MONDO NOVO

Rio de S. M. Formosa

C. DEI STAGNERI

Campo de la Fava

SANTA MARIA FAVA

C. MEZO

To San Marco

To San Marco

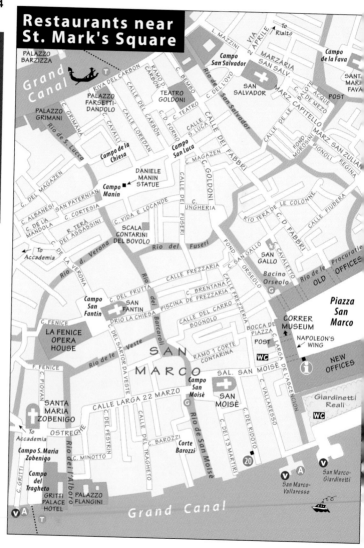

Restaurants near St. Mark's Square

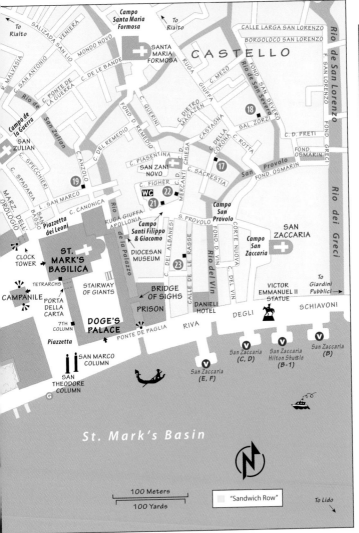

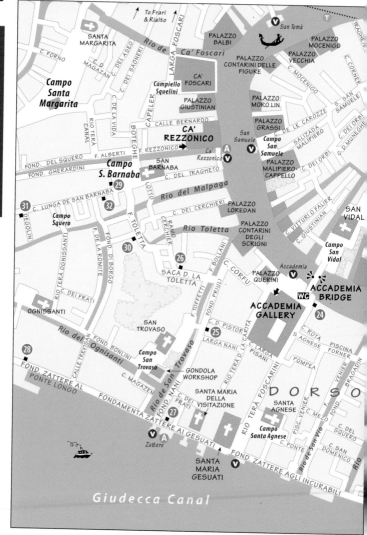

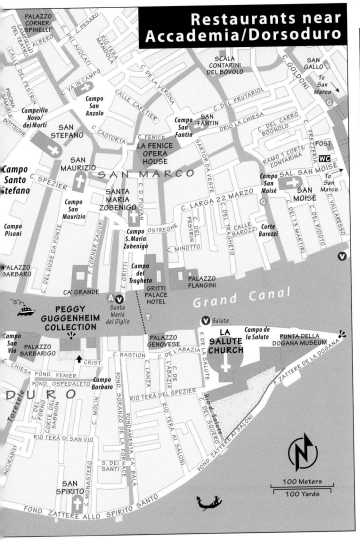

Restaurants near Accademia/Dorsoduro

EATING

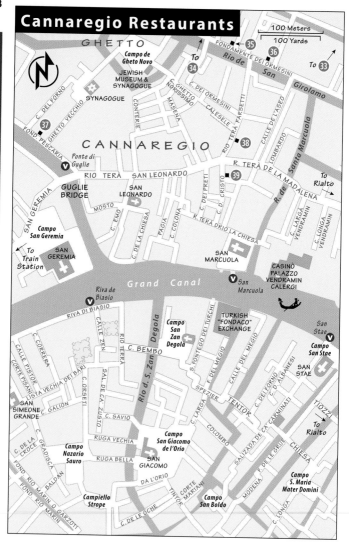

Cannaregio Restaurants

100 Meters

100 Yards

GHETTO

Campo de
Gheto Novo

To 34

FONDAMENTE DEI ORMESINI 35

36

Rio de

San

To 33

JEWISH
MUSEUM &
SYNAGOGUE

Girolamo

C. DEL FORNO

SYNAGOGUE

C. DEI ORMESINI

GHETTO
NUOVISSIMO

C. TERA FARSETTI

CALLE DE L'ASEO

Santa Marcuola

CONTERIE

GHETTO VECCHIO

CALESELE

MASENA

37

CANNAREGIO

38

LOMBARDO

FOND. PESCARIA

Ponte di
Guglie

RIO TERA SAN LEONARDO

RIO TERA DE LA MADALENA

V

39

To
Rialto

R. de

GUGLIE
BRIDGE

SAN
LEONARDO

C. DEI PRETI

C. D. CRISTO

MOSTO

C. EMO

PAGIA

C. COLONA

C. DE LA CHIESA

R. TERA DRIO LA CHIESA

C. LARGA
VENDRAMIN

C. LONGA
VENDRAMIN

San Geremia

Campo
San Geremia

SAN
GEREMIA

SAN
MARCUOLA

CASINO
PALAZZO
VENDRAMIN
CALERGI

To
Train
Station

Grand Canal

V San
Marcuola

Riva de
Biasio

V

RIVA DI BIASIO

Degola

Campo
San
Zan
Degola

TURKISH
"FONDACO"
EXCHANGE

San
Stae

V

CALLE ZEN

C. BEMBO

RIO TERRA

S. FONTEGO DEI TURCHI

CALLE DEL MEGIO

S. DEL MEGIO

Campo
San Stae

C. CORRERA

CORTE PISANI

SAL. DE CA' ZUSTO

Rio d. S. Zan

SPEZIER

TENTOR

C. DEL FORNO

C. D. ALBANESI

SAN
STAE

SAN
SIMEONE
GRANDE

CALLE VECHIA DEI BARI

C. ORSETI

C. GALION

C. SAVIO

C. LARGA

COLOMBO

SALIZADA DE CA' CARMINATI

F. DE LE GRUE

CHIESA

TIOZZI

To
Rialto

C. DE LA
CROCE

C. GRADISCA

RUGA VECHIA

Campo
San Giacomo
de l'Orio

MODENA

Campo
S. Maria
Mater Domini

FOND. RIO MARIN

BALDAN

Campo
Nazario
Sauro

RUGA BELLA

SAN
GIACOMO

DA L'ORIO

CORTE
MARIANI

C. LONGA

FOND. RIO MARIN O GARZOTI

Campiello
Strope

TINTOR

Campo
San Boldo

C. DE LE OCHE

Practicalities

HELPFUL HINTS

Travel Tips

Travel Advisories: Before traveling, check updated health and safety conditions, including restrictions for your destination, on the travel pages of the US State Department (www.travel.state.gov) and Centers for Disease Control and Prevention (www.cdc.gov/travel).

Tourist Information: Before your trip, scan the website of the Italian national tourist office (www.italia.it) for a wealth of travel information. If you have a specific question, try contacting one of their US offices (New York: +1 212 245 5618, newyork@enit.it; Los Angeles: +1 310 820 1898, losangeles@enit.it). **Venice TIs** are generally understaffed and not very helpful.

Time Zones: Venice is six/nine hours ahead of the East/West Coasts of the US. For a handy time converter, use the world clock app on your phone or download one (see www.timeanddate.com).

Business Hours: Most businesses are open Monday through Saturday, generally 9:00 to 13:00 and from 15:30-16:00 to 19:00-19:30. Many shops stay open through lunch or later into the evening, especially larger stores. In Venice, some stores and restaurants close on Sunday, or at least one other day per week.

Hurdling the Language Barrier: Many Italians—especially those in the tourist trade and in big cities—speak English. Still, you'll get better treatment if you learn and use Italian pleasantries. Italians have an endearing habit of talking to you even if they know you don't speak their language—and yet, thanks to gestures and thoughtfully simplified words, it somehow works. Don't stop them to tell them you don't understand every word—just go along for the ride. For a list of survival phrases, see page 205.

Watt's Up: Europe's electrical system is 220 volts, instead of North America's 110 volts. Most electronics (laptops, phones, cameras) and appliances (newer hair dryers, CPAP machines) convert automatically, so you won't need a converter, but you will need an adapter plug with two round prongs, sold inexpensively at travel stores in the US.

Safety and Emergencies

Emergency and Medical Help: For any emergency service—ambulance, police, or fire—call **112** from a mobile phone or landline. If you get sick, do as the locals do and go to a pharmacist for advice. Or ask at

Helpful Websites

Italian Tourist Information: Italia.it
Venice Tourist Information: VeneziaUnica.it
Other Helpful Venice Websites: VisitMuve.it (city-run museums), UnOspiteDiVenezia.it/en (sights and events), VeniceExplorer.com (mapping), and VeniceforVisitors.com.
Passports and Red Tape: Travel.state.gov
Cheap Flights: Kayak.com (international flights), Skyscanner.com (flights within Europe)
Airline Carry-on Restrictions: TSA.gov
European Train Schedules: Bahn.com
General Travel Tips: RickSteves.com (train travel, rail passes, car rental, travel insurance, packing lists, and much more)

your hotel for help—they'll know the nearest medical and emergency services.

Theft or Loss: While the dark, late-night streets of Venice are generally safe, pickpockets (often elegantly dressed) work all the extremely crowded areas: main streets, docks, and vaporetti. Be particularly careful at St. Mark's Square, near the Accademia or Rialto bridges, or on a tightly packed vaporetto.

A handy *polizia* station is on the right side of St. Mark's Square as you face the basilica (at #63, near Caffè Florian).

To replace a **passport,** you'll need to go in person to an embassy (in Rome—+39 06 46741, passport and nonemergency consular services, by appointment only, Via Vittorio Veneto 121). If your **credit and debit cards** disappear, cancel and replace them, and report the loss immediately (with a mobile phone, call these 24-hour US numbers: Visa—+1 303 967 1096, MasterCard—+1 636 722 7111, and American Express—+1 336 393 1111). For more information, see RickSteves.com/help.

Around Town

Bookstores: The well-stocked **Studium,** a block behind St. Mark's Basilica, sells new English books (Mon-Sat 9:30-19:30, shorter hours Sun, on Calle de la Canonica at #337—see map on page 33, +39 041 522 2382).

Funky **Acqua Alta** ("high water") bookstore displays books in a selection of vessels, including bathtubs and a gondola (daily 9:00-19:30, just beyond Campo Santa Maria Formosa on Lunga Santa Maria Formosa, Castello 5176, +39 041 296 0841). Or try **Libreria Marco Polo** on Campo Santa Margherita (Tue-Sat 11:00-13:00 & 15:00-19:00, closed Sun-Mon, Dorsoduro 2915, +39 041 822 4843).

Maps: Venice demands a good map. Hotels give away freebies, and TIs and some vaporetto ticket booths sell decent maps—but you can find a wider range at bookshops, newsstands, and postcard stands. Getting a map that shows all the tiny alleys may be the best money you spend in Venice, but many just rely on Google Maps and do fine.

Laundry: Across the Grand Canal from the train station is the coin-operated **Orange Self-Service Lavanderia** (daily 7:30-23:00, on Ramo de le Chioverete, Santa Croce 665a, mobile +39 346 972 5446). These places are near St. Mark's Square: self-service **Effe Erre** (daily 6:30-23:30, on Ruga Giuffa, Castello 4826, +39 340 712 5290); and **Lavanderia Gabriella** (drop off Mon-Fri 8:00-12:30, closed Sat-Sun; pick up 2 hours later or next working day, on Rio Terà de le Colonne, San Marco 985, +39 041 522 1758).

ARRIVAL IN VENICE

Marco Polo Airport

Venice's large, modern airport is on the mainland shore of the lagoon, six miles north of the city (code: VCE, www.veniceairport.it). There's one sleek terminal, with a TI (daily 9:00-20:00), car-rental agencies, ATMs, a bank, and plenty of shops and eateries.

You can get between the airport and central Venice by Alilaguna boat, water taxi, or airport bus. Allow plenty of time for the trip (which can easily take two hours).

Note that both Alilaguna boats and water taxis leave from the airport's boat dock, a 15-minute walk from the terminal. To get there, follow signs along a sleek series of (indoor) moving sidewalks.

Alilaguna Airport Boats (Slow but Easy): These boats make the scenic journey across the lagoon (€15, €27 round-trip, €1 more if bought on boat, includes 1 suitcase and 1 piece of hand luggage, additional bags €3 each, roughly 2/hour, 1-1.5-hour trip depending on destination, see www.alilaguna.it for schedule). Alilaguna boats are

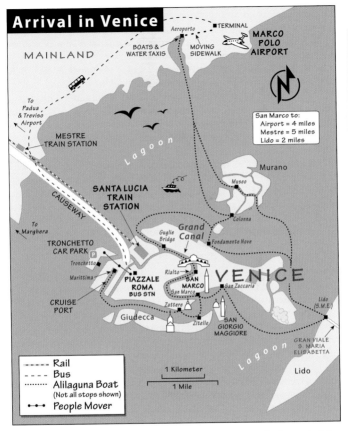

Arrival in Venice

not covered by city transit passes but use the same docks and ticket windows as the regular vaporetti.

Three key Alilaguna lines reach St. Mark's Square. The **orange line** (*linea arancio*) runs down the Grand Canal, reaching Guglie (handy for Cannaregio, 45 minutes), Rialto (1 hour), and San Marco (1.25 hours). The **blue line** (*linea blu*) heads first to Fondamente Nove (40 minutes), then loops around to San Zaccaria and San Marco (about

1.5 hours) before continuing to Zattere and the cruise terminal (almost 2 hours). In high season, if it's running, the **red line** (*linea rossa*) goes to St. Mark's in just over an hour (may be suspended—check online), ending at the cruise terminal.

Water Taxis (Fast but Pricey): Luxury taxi speedboats zip directly between the airport and the closest dock to your hotel, getting you within steps of your destination in about 30 minutes. The official price is €130 for up to four people; add €10 for every extra person (9-passenger limit). You may get a higher quote—politely talk it down. A taxi can be a smart investment for small groups and those with an early departure.

From the airport, arrange your ride at the water-taxi desk or with the boat captains at the dock. From Venice, book your taxi trip the day before your departure, either through your hotel or directly with the Consorzio Motoscafi water taxi association (Mon-Fri call +39 041 240 6712, Sat-Sun call +39 041 522 2303, www.motoscafivenezia.it).

Airport Shuttle Buses (Cheap but Less Direct): Buses from the airport drop you at Venice's bus station, at the square called Piazzale Roma. From there, you can catch a vaporetto down the Grand Canal. Two equally good bus companies serve this route. ATVO buses take 20 minutes and go nonstop; ACTV buses make a few stops en route and take slightly longer (30 minutes), but you get a discount if you buy a Venice vaporetto pass at the same time (either bus: €8 one-way, €15 round-trip; ACTV bus with transit-pass discount: €6 one-way, €12 round-trip; runs about 5:00-24:00, 2/hour, drops to 1/hour early and late, check schedules at www.atvo.it or www.actv.it).

Buses leave from just outside the airport arrivals terminal. Buy tickets from the TI, the ticket desk in the terminal, the kiosk near baggage claim, or ticket machines. ATVO tickets are not valid on ACTV buses and vice versa. Double-check the destination; you want Piazzale Roma. If taking ACTV, you want bus #5.

From Piazzale Roma, buy your ticket from the ACTV windows (in the building by the bridge) or the ATVO office (at #497g) before heading out to the platforms (although sometimes an attendant sells tickets near the buses). The newsstand in the center of the lot also sells tickets.

Santa Lucia Train Station

This station is located at the head of the Grand Canal, an easy vaporetto-ride or fascinating 45-minute walk (with a number of bridges and steps) to St. Mark's Square. (Don't confuse Santa Lucia station—called "Venezia S.L."—with Venezia Mestre on the mainland.)

The station has **baggage storage** (along track 1). Pay **WCs** are at track 1 and in the back of the big bar/cafeteria area in front of track 3. The **TI** is across from track 2.

Italy has two train companies: Trenitalia, with most connections (+39 06 6847 5475, www.trenitalia.it), and Italo, with high-speed routes between larger cities (no rail passes accepted, +39 06 8937 1892, www.italotreno.it). It's quick and easy to buy tickets online or with the Trenitalia app. If you buy tickets at the station, take advantage of the ticket (*biglietti*) machines that display schedules and issue tickets. For help, there's a ticket office in the corner near track 14.

The Ferrovia **vaporetto docks** are right outside the station's front door. There are five docks. Most tourists want the fast boats #2 or #2/ down the Grand Canal to Rialto (generally from dock B; #2/ goes only as far as Rialto; #2 continues to San Marco late May-mid-Sept) or the slow boat #1 down the Grand Canal, making every stop all the way to Rialto and San Marco (usually dock E).

A **water taxi** from the train station to central Venice costs about €70-80 (the taxi dock is to the left of the vaporetto docks).

Piazzale Roma Bus Station

Venice's "bus station" is at an open-air parking lot located at the head of the Grand Canal. The square itself is a jumble of different operators, platforms, and crosswalks over busy lanes of traffic. For buses to the airport, find the ticket windows for ACTV (in a building near the modern Calatrava Bridge and the vaporetto stop) or ATVO (#497g in the big, white building, on the right side of the square as you face away from the canal).

Piazzale Roma also has two big parking garages and the People Mover monorail (€1.50, links to the cruise port and then the parking-lot island of Tronchetto). A baggage-storage office is next to the monorail at #497m.

The vaporetto docks are just left of the modern bridge (take slow #1 or faster #2 down the Grand Canal to reach Rialto, Accademia, or San Marco stops).

Parking Garages

The freeway dead-ends after crossing the causeway to Venice. At the end of the road you have two parking-garage choices: Tronchetto or Piazzale Roma. As you approach, signs indicate which lots are full.

Tronchetto is a bit farther out, but it's cheaper than the garages at Piazzale Roma, well connected by vaporetto, and with 3,000 spaces, most likely to have a spot (€3-5/hour, €22/24 hours, +39 041 520 7555, www.veniceparking.it). From the garage, cross the street to the brick building and go right to the vaporetto dock (not well signed, look for *ACTV*). At the dock, catch vaporetto #2 in one of two directions: via the Grand Canal as far as Piazzale Roma (10 minutes), where you can transfer to line #2/ (express to the train station and Rialto) or line #1 for other Grand Canal destinations; or via Giudecca to San Marco/San Zaccaria (30 minutes).

Avoid aggressive water-taxi boatmen looking to overcharge, and travel agencies masquerading as TIs; deal only with the ticket booth at the vaporetto dock or the VèneziaUnica public transport office. The €1.50 **People Mover** monorail goes to the bus bays at Piazzale Roma.

Piazzale Roma's two garages are more convenient but more expensive and likelier to be full (you can reserve ahead online). Autorimessa Comunale city garage is in a big white building (at the end of the bridge before you get to the piazza, €26/24 hours, +39 041 272 7211, www.avmspa.it); the private Garage San Marco is in a back corner of the square (€45/24 hours, +39 041 523 2213, www.garagesanmarco.it).

Cruise Ports

As of 2022, larger ships dock at the commercial Marghera port outside of Venice, or at ports in Trieste or Ravenna, and transfer passengers by bus to Venice's Stazione Marittima, at the west end of town. (Some smaller cruise ships dock directly at Stazione Marittima.) From Stazione Marittima, if it's running, the most direct way to reach St. Mark's Square is to take the Alilaguna **red line** (www.alilaguna.it). Otherwise, walk five minutes to the **People Mover** monorail for a three-minute ride to Piazzale Roma, then hop on a **vaporetto.** Or take an expensive **water taxi** ride (at least €70-80).

GETTING AROUND VENICE

On Foot

The city's "streets" are narrow pedestrian walkways connecting its docks, squares, bridges, and courtyards. To navigate, look for signs on street corners pointing you to (*per*) the nearest major landmark: San Marco (St. Mark's Square), Rialto (the bridge), Accademia (another bridge), Ferrovia (literally "railroad," meaning the train station), and Piazzale Roma (the bus station).

Helpful Terminology: *Campo* means square, a *campiello* is a small square, *calle* (pronounced "KAH-lay" with an "L" sound) means street, and *ponte* is a bridge. A *fondamenta* is the embankment along a canal or the lagoon. A *rio terà* is a street that was once a canal and has been filled in. A *sotoportego* is a covered passageway.

Don't worry about getting lost. When it comes time to find your way, just follow the signs or simply ask a local, *"Dov'è San Marco?"* ("Where is St. Mark's?")

By Vaporetto

These motorized boats, run by a company called ACTV, work like city buses except they never get a flat, the stops are docks, and if you jump off between stops, you might drown. For schedules and general information about the vaporetti, see www.actv.it or www.veneziaunica.it.

Tickets and Passes: A single ticket costs €9.50 and is good for 75 minutes of one-way travel; you can hop on and off at stops and change boats during that time. Or you can buy a pass: €25/24 hours, €35/48 hours, €45/72 hours, €65/7-day pass. These passes pay for themselves in a hurry, so think through your Venice itinerary before you pay for your first vaporetto trip. On the other hand, many tourists just walk and rarely use a boat.

Purchase tickets and passes from the machines at most stops, from ticket windows (at larger stops), or from the VèneziaUnica offices at the train station, bus station, and Tronchetto parking lot. If you're unable to purchase a ticket before boarding, buy one from the conductor when you board (or risk a hefty fine).

Riding the Vaporetto: Before you board, validate your ticket or pass by touching it to the small white pad on the dock until you hear a pinging sound (you need to touch the pass each time you board a boat).

The machine readout shows how long your ticket is valid—and inspectors do come by now and then to check tickets.

For most travelers, only a few vaporetto lines matter. **Line #1** leaves every 10 minutes or so and goes up and down the Grand Canal, between the "mouth" of the fish at one end and St. Mark's Square at the other. Making every stop along the way, it takes 45 minutes to complete the full route. **Line #2** runs between Piazzale Roma (bus station) and San Marco/San Zaccaria via Giudecca (35 minutes); the companion **line #2/** goes from Piazzale Roma to Ferrovia (train station) and Rialto via the Grand Canal (10 minutes). From late May to mid-September, line #2 also runs an express route up and down the Grand Canal, between Piazzale Roma and San Marco/San Zaccaria (35 minutes).

Handy Vaporetti from San Zaccaria: About 150 yards east of St. Mark's square are the four San Zaccaria docks, where several helpful boats depart:

- **Line #1** goes up the Grand Canal. In the other direction, it goes east to Arsenale, Giardini, and Lido.
- **Line #2** goes up the Grand Canal. In the other direction, it zips over to San Giorgio Maggiore.
- **Lines #4.1 and #7** go to Murano in 45 and 25 minutes, respectively.
- **Lines #5.1 and #5.2** make a circular loop around the island—perfect if you just like riding boats.
- The **Alilaguna Shuttle Boat** running to and from the airport stops here.

By *Traghetto*

These gondola-like, oar-powered boats shuttle locals and in-the-know tourists across the Grand Canal. (Find the stops on the map on page 18.) Just step in, hand the gondolier €2, and enjoy the ride—standing or sitting. Some *traghetti* are seasonal, some stop running as early as 12:30, and all stop by 18:00. *Traghetti* are not covered by any transit pass.

By Water Taxi

Venetian taxis, like speedboat limos, hang out at busy points along the Grand Canal. Prices are regulated and fixed by destination (for

Tipping

Tipping in Italy isn't as automatic and generous as it is in the US.

Restaurants: In Italy, a service charge (*servizio*) is usually built into your check (look at the bill carefully). If it is included, there's no need to leave an extra tip. If it's not included, it's common to leave about €1 per person (a bit more at finer restaurants) or to round up the bill. If paying with a credit card, be prepared to tip separately with cash or coins; credit card receipts often don't have a tip line.

Taxis: For a typical ride, round up your fare a bit (for instance, if the fare is €4.50, pay €5).

Services: In general, if someone in the tourism or service industry does a super job for you, a small tip of a euro or two is appropriate...but not required.

example, the 20-minute trip from the train station to San Marco costs €70). Despite regulation, prices can be soft; negotiate and settle on the price or rate before stepping in. For travelers with lots of luggage or small groups who can split the cost, taxi-boat rides can be a worthwhile and time-saving convenience—and skipping across the lagoon in a classic wooden motorboat is a cool indulgence. For about €120 an hour, you can have a private, unguided taxi-boat tour. You may find more competitive rates if you prebook through the Consorzio Motoscafi water taxi association (prices good for up to 4 people, 1 bag/person, extra passengers €10 each, maximum 9 people, extra fees for late night and extra bags, +39 041 522 2303, www.motoscafivenezia.it).

MONEY

Italy uses the euro currency: 1 euro (€) = about $1.10. To convert prices in euros to dollars, add about 10 percent: €20 = about $22, €50 = about $55. (Check www.oanda.com for the latest exchange rates.)

You'll use your **credit card** for purchases both big (hotels, advance tickets) and small (little shops, food stands). A "tap-to-pay" or "contactless" card is the most widely accepted and simplest to use.

Get comfortable using **contactless pay** options. Check to see if you already have—or can get—a tap-to-pay version of your credit card (look on the card for the tap-to-pay symbol—four curvy lines). Make sure you know the numeric, four-digit PIN for each of your cards, both debit and credit. Request it if you don't have one, as it may be required for some purchases.

Use a **debit card** at ATMs (*bancomat*) to withdraw a small amount of local cash. While most transactions are by card these days, cash can help you out of a jam if your card randomly doesn't work, and can be useful to pay for things like tips and local guides. Keep your cards and cash safe in a **money belt.**

At self-service payment machines (such as transit-ticket kiosks), US cards may not work. In this case, look for a cashier who can process your card manually—or pay in cash.

STAYING CONNECTED

Making International Calls

From a Mobile Phone: Phone numbers in this book are presented exactly as you would dial them from a US mobile phone. For international access, press and hold 0 (zero) to get a + sign, then dial the country code (39 for Italy) and phone number.

From a US Landline to Europe: Replace + with 011 (US/Canada access code), then dial the country code (39 for Italy) and phone number.

From a European Landline to the US or Europe: Replace + with 00 (Europe access code), then dial the country code (39 for Italy, 1 for the US) and phone number. For more phoning help, see HowToCallAbroad.com.

Using Your Phone in Europe

Sign up for an international plan. To stay connected at a lower cost, sign up for an international service plan through your carrier. Most providers offer a simple bundle that includes calling, messaging, and data.

Use free Wi-Fi whenever possible. Unless you have an unlimited-data plan, save most of your online tasks for Wi-Fi. Most accommodations in Europe offer free Wi-Fi, and many cafés offer hotspots for customers. You may also find Wi-Fi at TIs, city squares, major museums, public-transit hubs, airports, and aboard trains and buses.

Minimize use of your cellular network. Even with an international data plan, wait until you're on Wi-Fi to Skype or FaceTime, download apps, stream videos, or do other megabyte-greedy tasks. Using a navigation app such as Google Maps over a cellular network can require lots of data, so download maps when you're on Wi-Fi, then use the app offline.

Use Wi-Fi calling and messaging apps. Skype, WhatsApp, FaceTime, and Google Meet are great for making free or low-cost calls or sending texts over Wi-Fi worldwide.

RESOURCES FROM RICK STEVES

Begin your trip at RickSteves.com: This book is just one of many in my series on European travel. I also produce a public television series, *Rick Steves' Europe,* and a public radio show, *Travel with Rick Steves.* My mobile-friendly website is *the* place to explore Europe in preparation for your trip. You'll find thousands of fun articles, videos, and radio interviews; a wealth of money-saving tips; travel news dispatches; a video library of travel talks; my travel blog; our latest guidebook updates (RickSteves.com/update); and the free Rick Steves Audio Europe app with audio tours of Europe's top sights. You can also follow me on Facebook, Instagram, and Twitter.

INDEX

Start your trip at

Our website enhances this book and turns

Explore Europe

At ricksteves.com you can browse through thousands of articles, videos, photos and radio interviews, plus find a wealth of money-saving travel tips for planning your dream trip. And with our mobile-friendly website, you can easily access all this great travel information anywhere you go.

TV Shows

Preview the places you'll visit by watching entire half-hour episodes of *Rick Steves' Europe* (choose from all 100 shows) on-demand, for free.

ricksteves.com

your travel dreams into affordable reality

Radio Interviews

Enjoy ready access to Rick's vast library of radio interviews covering travel tips and cultural insights that relate specifically to your Europe travel plans.

Travel Forums

Learn, ask, share! Our online community of savvy travelers is a great resource for first-time travelers to Europe, as well as seasoned pros.

Travel News

Subscribe to our free Travel News e-newsletter, and get monthly updates from Rick on what's happening in Europe.

Classroom Europe®

Check out our free resource for educators with 500 short video clips from the *Rick Steves' Europe* TV show.

Audio Europe™

Rick's Free Travel App

Get your FREE Rick Steves Audio Europe™ app to enjoy...

- Dozens of self-guided tours of Europe's top museums, sights and historic walks

- Hundreds of tracks filled with cultural insights and sightseeing tips from Rick's radio interviews

- All organized into handy geographic playlists

- For Apple and Android

With Rick whispering in your ear, Europe gets even better.

Find out more at ricksteves.com

Pack Light and Right

Gear up for your next adventure at ricksteves.com

Light Luggage

Pack light and right with Rick Steves' affordable, custom-designed rolling carry-on bags, backpacks, day packs and shoulder bags.

Accessories

From packing cubes to moneybelts and beyond, Rick has personally selected the travel goodies that will help your trip go smoother.

Shop at ricksteves.com

Rick Steves has

Experience maximum Europe

Save time and energy

This guidebook is your independent-travel toolkit. But for all it delivers, it's still up to you to devote the time and energy it takes to manage the preparation and logistics that are essential for a happy trip. If that's a hassle, there's a solution.

Rick Steves Tours

A Rick Steves tour takes you to Europe's most interesting places with great guides and small groups.

great tours, too!

with minimum stress

We follow Rick's favorite itineraries, ride in comfy buses, stay in family-run hotels, and bring you intimately close to the Europe you've traveled so far to see. Most importantly, we take away the logistical headaches so you can focus on the fun.

Join the fun

This year we'll take thousands of free-spirited travelers—nearly half of them repeat customers—along with us on four dozen different itineraries, from Ireland to Italy to Athens. Is a Rick Steves tour the right fit for your travel dreams? Find out at ricksteves.com, where you can check seat availability and sign up.

Europe is best experienced with happy travel partners. We hope you can join us.

See our itineraries at ricksteves.com

A Guide for Every Trip

BEST OF GUIDES
Full-color guides in an easy-to-scan format, focusing on top sights and experiences in popular destinations

Best of England
Best of Europe
Best of France
Best of Germany

Best of Ireland
Best of Italy
Best of Scotland
Best of Spain

COMPREHENSIVE GUIDES
City, country, and regional guides printed on Bible-thin paper. Packed with detailed coverage for a multi-week trip exploring iconic sights and more

Amsterdam &
  the Netherlands
Barcelona
Belgium: Bruges, Brussels,
  Antwerp & Ghent
Berlin
Budapest
Croatia & Slovenia
Eastern Europe
England
Florence & Tuscany
France
Germany
Great Britain
Greece: Athens &
  the Peloponnese
Iceland

Ireland
Istanbul
Italy
London
Paris
Portugal
Prague & the Czech Republic
Provence & the French
  Riviera
Rome
Scandinavia
Scotland
Sicily
Spain
Switzerland
Venice
Vienna, Salzburg & Tirol

Many guides are available as ebooks.

PHOTO CREDITS

Avalon Travel
Hachette Book Group
1700 Fourth Street
Berkeley, CA 94710

Printed in Malaysia for Imago
Fifth Edition
First printing October 2023

ISBN 978-1-64171-569-0

For the latest on Rick's talks, guidebooks, tours, public television series, and public radio show, contact Rick Steves' Europe, 130 Fourth Avenue North, Edmonds, WA 98020, +1 425 771 8303, RickSteves.com, rick@ricksteves.com.

Rick Steves' Europe
Managing Editor: Jennifer Madison Davis
Assistant Managing Editor: Cathy Lu
Editors: Glenn Eriksen, Tom Griffin, Suzanne Kotz, Rosie Leutzinger, Teresa Nemeth, Jessica Shaw, Carrie Shepherd, Chelsea Wing
Graphic Content Director: Sandra Hundacker
Maps & Graphics: Orin Dubrow, David C. Hoerlein, Lauren Mills, Mary Rostad

Avalon Travel
Senior Editor and Series Manager: Madhu Prasher
Associate Managing Editors: Jamie Andrade, Sierra Machado
Copy Editor: Jennifer Malnick
Proofreader: Kelly Lydick
Indexer: Claire Splan
Production & Typesetting: Rue Flaherty
Cover Design: Kimberly Glyder Design
Interior Design: Darren Alessi
Maps & Graphics: Kat Bennett